Jane Williams was born in India, of missionary parents, and is one of five sisters. She took a degree in theology at Cambridge and has worked in theological publishing and in Christian adult education. Her most recent job was as lecturer and doctrine tutor at Trinity College, Bristol. Her publications include *Bread, Wine and Women* (with Sue Dowell), *Perfect Freedom* and *Lectionary Reflections, Year C*. She is married and has two school-aged children.

Lectionary Reflections

Year A

———— ∾ ————

Jane Williams

First published in Great Britain in 2004 by
Society for Promoting Christian Knowledge
Holy Trinity Church
Marylebone Road
London NW1 4DU

British Library Cataloguing-in-Publication Data
A catalogue record for this book is available from the British Library

ISBN 0–281–05527–0

1 3 5 7 9 10 8 6 4 2

Typeset by Avocet Typeset, Chilton, Aylesbury, Bucks
Printed in Great Britain by Ashford Colour Press

Contents

— ~ —

Preface

—— ≈ ——

These pieces originally appeared in the *Church Times* as a regular 'Sunday Readings' column. I am very grateful to Paul Handley, Rachel Boulding and the other staff at the paper for the opportunity and the support they offered. I am not a biblical scholar, and took on the task with some trepidation, but have been encouraged by many generous readers of the *Church Times* to think that these reflections may help preachers and congregations to engage with and enjoy the Sunday lectionary readings assigned for use with *Common Worship*.

Advent

The First Sunday of Advent

———— ∾ ————

Isaiah 2.1–5
Romans 13.11–14
Matthew 24.36–44

In *The Magician's Nephew*, one of his Narnia books, C. S. Lewis describes a wood, which the children reach by magic. It is a kind of no-place, which Polly and Diggory come to call 'the Wood between the Worlds'. From that place they enter Charn, a dying world, Narnia at the dawn of its creation, and return again, at last, to their own world. But in the wood, time is suspended, and they can hardly begin to imagine the trials and adventures that await them in the many different worlds they are to visit.[1]

Advent is a 'wood between the worlds'. It is a point in the Christian calendar where we stand between two worlds: the world that cannot imagine Christ, and the world in which he comes to be the only picture of reality we have. At this point, we stand in a world where God's great act of incarnation and redemption is just a shadow, a child growing in the womb, secretly, in the dark. We do not know yet what this child will be like, or what his impact on our lives will be.

So Advent is a time of preparing to choose again. Which world will we choose? Will we choose the world of the newly born child, where so many of our most dearly held ideas about God and ourselves will be challenged? Or will we choose the old world, where there is no life, no birth, but at least there is also no challenge?

The 'wood between the worlds' is a place of great drowsiness because it is not a real place, and both Romans and Matthew warn us that the danger of the waiting period is sleep, oblivion, unpreparedness.

Matthew reminds us that it is very easy to live as though our world is real and secure, and as though there is no need to be

---

[1] C. S. Lewis, *The Magician's Nephew*, The Bodley Head, 1955.

watchful or poised for action. Until the moment they were swept away by the flood, the people of Noah's day were carrying on their normal lives, oblivious to the frantic hammering and animal-herding that was going on in Noah's back yard. Only Noah was prepared for what happened. All the little vignettes Matthew paints, of people innocently getting on with their lives, or turning their backs at just the wrong moment – any one of those could be us, Matthew says.

Paul, too, warns of the dangers of dozing off during this vital period when we need to prepare to make life-and-death decisions. Being Paul, he does not like to admit ignorance, as Matthew does, of when the time will come. Instead, he urges us to get ready for the dawn – it's time to be polishing our armour so that it will gleam in the sun that is about to rise. Don't go back to sleep now: any minute the alarm will go off.

But if Matthew and Paul are proper Advent readings, with their emphasis on the importance of preparation, Isaiah reminds us what it is all for. Although the centre of these verses is the vision of the Lord's house, restored to its proper focal position, our eyes are drawn to the people streaming towards the holy mountain. What are they looking for? Why have they come? They are, apparently, people who are sick of war, and who know that they have lost any ability to judge whether or not the fight is just. They long for an arbiter, they long for peace and above all they long to learn a new way of living (v. 3). They are people who have learned the hard way the cost of wrong choices, and now they ache to be taught, to be prepared for a different world.

But Isaiah's own longing is betrayed in the last verse of this reading. 'O house of Jacob,' he pleads, 'come, let *us* walk in the light of the LORD.' Surely, surely, he begs, we can see what God is offering? If even the nations, who have not known God, can look to him and see him as their heart's desire, surely we, his people, can admit that this is the way of life. Indeed, perhaps the two are connected. Perhaps if we, God's people, prepare ourselves to walk in his light, we will make the path plain for others who are lost and longing. Or is it, shamingly, sometimes the other way round? Will perhaps the desperate, those utterly despairing of the world they know, lead us, who are supposed to be God's people, to his path?

Choosing between worlds is not easy. It needs to be prepared for and imagined, over and over again. When the child is born, will it be a shock of anguish or of joy?

The Second Sunday of Advent

———— ❧ ————

Isaiah 11.1–10
Romans 15.4–13
Matthew 3.1–12

Paul's letter to the Romans is the most formal that he wrote. He is writing to a church that he does not know, and in whose setting up and history he has not played a part. But he is writing as one already known to them, by reputation, to announce that he hopes to pay them a visit. Since it is not written in the midst of white-hot pastoral crises or violent controversies, Paul is able to sit back a bit and write reflectively about the theological conclusions that his calling as apostle to the Gentiles have forced upon him over the years. The result is a great testimony to God's determination to save us, and it has inspired Christians throughout the centuries. Theologians of all generations have written commentaries on it. Arguably, it was the cause of Martin Luther's breakthrough, in the sixteenth century, into belief in God's forgiving love. He wrote that he longed to believe what he read in Romans, that faith is all God asks. In the first decades of the twentieth century, while writing a commentary on Romans, Karl Barth was reminded that we cannot domesticate God, who is sovereign, free and utterly beyond our petty religiosity.

So we come to the reading of Romans with this great cloud of witnesses, known and unknown, who have heard Paul's words as glorious good news. One of the great themes of Romans is that of God's faithfulness. Paul sets the redeeming work of God in Christ against the whole universal history of God's dealings with us, from creation onwards, to show that God faithfully, persistently, inexorably moves his saving work forward.

In a number of his letters, Paul worries away at the question of how God's old work and new work relate. In particular, how God's old covenant with his people relates to the new promises made to all in Jesus. This is clearly a personal question for him, since he was brought up as a devout and well-educated Jew, proud to be part of

4

God's covenant people (see Galatians 1. 13ff. for a bit of autobiography), and then became the leading evangelist to those outside the Jewish race. But today's reading is not concerned with his own tensions, but is a strong exhortation to unity, based upon God's own unifying vision, laid out in Scripture.

Paul is arguing that, if you see Jesus in the context of all that God has done in the past, you see the skilful weaving fingers of God, always building the diverse threads into a lovely pattern, and you see that all the pattern coalesces around that central figure of Christ. If you stand close, the colours around Christ blaze out, startlingly bright and new; if you stand back, however, you can see the reds and purples of his life gradually building, dimly traced, in the earlier pattern too.

In other places, Paul makes the same point by using the metaphor of the first and the last Adam (see Romans 5, 1 Corinthians 15). God does not drop threads, even if we, who are supposed to be helping him, keep pulling the pattern into the wrong shape. God still works our blunders into the pattern, and even uses them to point up the figure of Jesus in the middle.

But here in Romans 15, Paul is suggesting that we can learn to be more like God if we watch him at work. Just as he weaves everything together into one complex yet satisfying whole, so we, his people, can become apprentice weavers. But first, we have to learn to see the pattern, learn to see the strength and loveliness of weaving things together, rather than pulling them apart.

At the end of this section, Paul quotes from the Old Testament, from others who have realized that God's purpose is much bigger than you might think.

Isaiah, too, is exploring themes of faithfulness and novelty; he, too, has seen that God can do the stunningly unexpected things that turn out to make sense of all that has gone before. So it is from the same root as David that the new order is to spring. But if David's role was to be the King of Israel, his descendant's job is to bring all the peoples to God. Paul longs for the Christian community to see and mirror God's great unifying work, while Isaiah dreams of a time when the whole of creation will see that it is made to live in harmony. Creatures whose whole nature should set them at enmity will see God's righteousness and faithfulness (v. 5), and know peace.

So John the Baptist strides out of the desert, calling people to respond to God's great new action, which is his eternal action of love for what he has made.

The Third Sunday of Advent

—— ~ ——

Isaiah 35.1–10
James 5.7–10
Matthew 11.2–11

In last Sunday's Gospel reading (Matthew 3. 1–12), John the Baptist arrives to herald the beginning of Jesus's adult ministry. He is incredibly rude to the people who flock to hear him preach their judgement and downfall, and they just love it. But by this morning's Gospel reading, they have tired of him and the uncomfortable truths he tells, and he is in prison.

He sends some of his few remaining faithful followers to Jesus. Is he going to ask the new favourite to use his influence with the people to free John? Is he going to remind Jesus how much he owes to John, who was the first to recognize him and give him a helping hand up the ladder? Not at all. What John wants to know is whether it is safe for him to give up, to hand his mission on.

John has never been under any illusion about what he is. The centre of the stage is not for him. But equally, he does not undervalue what he is called to do. He is the one who is to herald the coming of God's Messiah, and he cannot relax until he knows whether or not he has done his job. So he sends to ask, 'Are you the one who is to come, or are we to wait for another?' (v. 3).

So when John's disciples carry Jesus's answer back to him, did he hear it as a yes or a no? What Jesus says could not be more different from the message that John preached. John shouted for repentance in the face of the wrath of God: he spoke of the axe cutting down the dead trees, and the unquenchable fire waiting for the empty husks from the threshing-floor. Jesus, on the other hand, speaks of mercy, healing and rejoicing. Did John recognize the connection? Did he see that the mercy Jesus is offering is as much a judgement on the world as the terrible fire that John himself envisaged? Did he see it as God's forceful overturning of the complacent values of those John called a 'brood of vipers'? Perhaps he did. He comes across as a man of very little personal vanity and a huge, fierce

6

commitment to God's kingdom, so perhaps he could let go of his own interpretation and rejoice in God's new work in Christ.

Matthew specifically tells us that John's disciples have gone to carry their odd message back to their master by the time Jesus pays tribute to John. All the reassurance he is to get is that cryptic message, which he must interpret in terms of his own knowledge of God. Jesus's witness to John and his message is not for John, to boost his ego, but for the crowds who once followed him, then transferred their allegiance to Jesus, and who will soon be looking for the next, more palatable, sensation.

The tribute that Jesus pays to John is warm, perceptive and puzzling. He firmly identifies John with the fulfilment of prophecy, and says he is the greatest man ever born. And yet, he is still outside. He is the messenger, not the message. He has to stand behind and point forward. We, who lack John's courage, his love of God and his calling, are on the inside, partly because he was prepared to play just that role and no other, bigger one.

But Jesus's message to John is not just a take-it-or-leave-it summary of Jesus's own ministry, but is in a code that Jesus is sure John will be able to read. Jesus is quoting from Isaiah 35, as John would surely have known, and the message is all about John. The wilderness, John's home, is to break into flower, the fearful are to be comforted. John is in prison, awaiting certain death; how can he not be afraid? John preached the judgement and vengeance of God, and here in Isaiah, God's wrath is an instrument of salvation for the weak and the fearful.

So when, at last, we come to the words that Jesus uses in today's Gospel, John will know that Jesus is talking about the continuation and fulfilment of his own message. John can be certain that Jesus is indeed the one he came to herald.

But now, in Advent, we cannot run too fast to reach that great highway of the ransomed of the Lord, where even those of us who are fools will not be able to get lost. Now is the time for patience, as James reminds us. As the 'early and late rains' (v. 7) fall on us, we begin to grow into the coming kingdom.

The Fourth Sunday of Advent

—— ∾ ——

Isaiah 7.10–16
Romans 1.1–7
Matthew 1.18–25

Why won't King Ahaz ask God for a sign? The reason he gives sounds like a good religious response, but the tone of the story makes it clear that it isn't. What he says is 'I will not put the Lord to the test' (v. 12). In the Gospels, we often see that Jesus is asked for a sign, and refuses to give one, so why is Ahaz not right to refuse to ask for a sign? The simple answer is that Ahaz is wrong because, in this case, God himself has told Ahaz to ask, so that Ahaz's refusal is a deliberate determination to turn his back on what God is offering.

This is the second time that God has spoken to Ahaz in the middle of the deep political crisis for his kingdom. Judah is the subject of a double-pronged attack, and Ahaz is very frightened. Two of the neighbouring kingdoms are trying to force Judah into an alliance against the king of Assyria. God has already told Ahaz that he has nothing to fear (cf. v. 4), but Ahaz does not believe God.

So when we come to today's readings, we see Ahaz's real reason for rejecting God – he no longer trusts. It is hard to tell which he fears most – that God will be proved wrong, or that God will make him change his mind. Because Ahaz has already decided what he will do – he will submit to the King of Assyria. He is going to put his trust in his own political intelligence rather than God, and he cannot risk letting God mess up his decision with signs. The result of Ahaz's failure of nerve is a sign that reverberates down the centuries, though Ahaz may never have understood it or seen its fulfilment.

Matthew picks up on this sign, and knows exactly how to interpret the young woman whose child is called 'God is with us'.

Joseph's encounter with the angel is told in very straightforward and pragmatic language. There are no bursts of blazing light, no drift of snow-white feathers, just Joseph asleep and dreaming. But his response to God is so different from Ahaz's. He simply, immediately, follows his dream, marries Mary, and steps into the story of the world's salvation. Ahaz chooses, though he doesn't know it, to step out of the light, into the background, so that he becomes just a sign of what is to take place without him. But Joseph's trust puts him at the heart of what God is doing in Jesus Christ.

It is hard to value Joseph properly. We get so few insights into his character, and the story could so clearly have gone ahead without him. But Matthew is prepared to give him his due. Joseph trusts God, simply and immediately, although it involves him in heartache and shame; and so Ahaz's rejected sign of the woman and child becomes a family, a trinity, a sign that human beings are capable of responding to each other and to God. In Matthew's account of the birth of Jesus, Joseph's role, as the one who listens to God and protects his family, is vital. Joseph's function is to be there for others, to forget himself and his needs and desires, and to make room for God's action in the woman and the child. Even before we know what the child will be, we can see the presence of God in Joseph's self-abnegation.

So although Paul makes no mention of Joseph, in Romans or anywhere else, still the mission that he accepts is not unlike Joseph's. Paul is to protect the Word of God and make room for it in the world. Paul is called to bear witness to that sign that Ahaz rejected and Matthew accepted, which is 'God with us'.

Thanks, at least partly, to Joseph's willingness to be nothing more nor less than God asks him to be, Paul, the Romans and we can see the fulfilment of prophecy. God is infinitely patient in doing what he has promised, and he never forgets. The promise made to David, rejected by Ahaz, misunderstood and misinterpreted by many others, comes to completion in Jesus. And as the promise waits, it grows and grows, to include more and more of us in its scope.

In this last week of Advent, we can stand either with Ahaz or with Joseph. Either we can refuse God's sign, the sign of the coming child, and step out of the story, handing on our part to someone braver and more trusting, or we can accept the call to protect the child and to help the world see him as the sign that 'God is with us'.

Christmas

Christmas Eve/Christmas Day

— ❧ —

Isaiah 9.2–7
Titus 2.11–14
Luke 2.1–20

Luke starts what is to be one of the world's most famous narratives on the world stage, as it is traditionally recounted. He starts with emperors and governors, who are, after all, the people who make history, aren't they? These gigantic figures decree and the little ant-like ordinary folk rush around madly in response to their orders. Augustus lifts a finger and the whole of the region is on the move. The roads are choked with slow-moving donkeys, impatient horses and carriages, trudging figures with bundles and wailing children, all off to be counted, because the Emperor and the Governor say so. That's power for you.

Luke then switches his focus to a different but equally vast stage. Now his scene is the sweep of Israel's history. Joseph goes, admittedly at the bidding of the rulers, but he goes as one who knows that he, too, represents history-makers, because he is a descendant of David. In the history of God's relationships with his people, David is pivotal, at least as important as any Roman emperor or governor.

So civil history and religious history are coming together to provide the gigantic backdrop, and we know that we are to witness something enormous. But then, hang on, whatever is going on? On to this massive stage comes a baby. The sense of anticlimax is huge. Everything is done to diminish this strange entrance of the principal character. His birth happens off stage, and he is shoved into a corner, because the stage is already full of other more important-looking people and events. We begin to get bewildered. History is being turned on its head.

Well, exactly. History *is* being turned on its head. The powerfully significant scenery of religious and political stature is quite proper – history is being changed here, but part of the change is in our under-standing of how momentous events are to be judged. From the moment this baby is born and wrapped in bands of cloth and put in a corner somewhere, corners and dark insignificant places take on a whole new meaning. Rulers and governors can shout away centre-stage all they like, but we begin to see that they may not be taking part in anything at all important. Whatever they may think, their reigns are ephemeral. They are no longer the ones who are shaping the world.

This is what the angels tell the astonished shepherds, which is, in itself, part of this strange shift in history. Why send your heavenly hosts to a group of shepherds? If they were to go to an emperor or a governor, they might even be able to get the baby a proper start in life, or at least a decent room and a cradle. But no, the angels are sent to the shepherds, so the shepherds are the first to learn that the world has changed for ever. 'And don't go mistaking the sign,' the angels warn the stunned shepherds. 'We are not the sign, for all our winged brightness. The baby is the sign. He is the symbol of salvation.'

Nothing could be clearer than this set of contrasts that Luke sees attending the birth of the one who is the Saviour. The huge machinery put into operation to get him to the right place at the right time, of the right ancestors. And then, when he arrives, he is born into obscurity. The massed choir of angels is sent to announce the news, but to shepherds, who will have no power to broadcast what they have been told.

It is as though God is saying, 'Things can only be changed this way. Power and might, grandeur and status, only perpetuate themselves and draw people further and further into the world they have made themselves, a world that clearly does not work. Only this can draw them out of themselves and make them look at the world I created, the real world.'

God's way to draw us back to the real aim of our existence is a strange way. He comes to live with us, as one of us, in utter humility. He is born in fragility and danger, as a human baby, with no wealth or power of privilege to protect him. All the trappings of earth and heaven are held at arm's length, so that Jesus can be just what we are, but so often refuse to be – fully human, dependent only upon God the Father.

This humility is to be the source of our new life, if we are humble enough to accept it. Our nourishment lies in the animal trough. This is the bread of life. Are we too grand to feed with the animals, or can we join the shepherds in rejoicing and 'praising God for all we have seen and heard'?

The First Sunday of Christmas

— ∽ —

Isaiah 63.7–9
Hebrews 2.10–18
Matthew 2.13–23

Isaiah and Hebrews show us God's way of being in the world, a way that should be blindingly obvious to us at Christmas.

Isaiah is reminding the people of all that God has done for them throughout the ages. But although he talks in general terms about God's 'praiseworthy acts' and 'great favour', the real cause of joy is not the deeds, but the presence of God himself with his people. Isaiah wants his people to remember, as though this is a formative memory from their childhood, the times when God has been with them, and shown them how much he loved and pitied them. They can almost feel again what it is like to be small enough and trusting enough to be carried on God's shoulders. It is as though God is a father and Israel a child, feeling the magical mixture of excitement and security that riding up so high on a father's shoulders can bring. This is what God offers his people, his own love and presence. And because he loves them, he makes himself vulnerable to them. They 'will not deal falsely', God thinks of his children, and he trusts himself and his message to them.

Through all the centuries that follow, when that trust proves false over and over again, God's purpose does not waver, and neither does his love. Still God gives himself to his people, and willingly risks what follows, until we reach the logical conclusion, here at Christmas time. God becomes a human being, sharing flesh and blood and suffering, to be with his people. God made us to share his life, but since we are too stupid or proud to see that, he comes instead and shares ours.

So Isaiah and Hebrews have an understanding of how God works. He desires closeness and intimacy. He works by sharing himself, trusting himself to us, long after we have, by all possible measures, proven ourselves untrustworthy. He is willing to be vulnerable, to see his plans apparently go awry, but still not to change direction, but patiently, persistently, unerringly to go on giving himself to us, finding new, creative, stunningly unexpected ways of offering us a share in his life.

Herod, on the other hand, chooses a different way of working. His way of bringing about what he longs for is to seize it by force, and without any concern for anyone else. Herod wants power, but he can never have enough of it. After all, he is already a king. Herod had options. He could, for example, have sought out the child and adopted it, thereby extending his own rule into the next generation. But such a thought never enters his head. Or he could have calculated his own age and that of the new-born child and reckoned on a good number of years still as king before the child could prove any threat to him. Or he could have looked at the three strange men who came looking for the new 'king' and simply laughed.

But because Herod's whole identity is bound up with his need for power, and because he trusts no one but himself to give him what he wants, he cannot see any of those options. And so he kills, madly and in vain, to try to get security for himself.

Rachel's weeping for her children is a sound that has echoed down the ages, and still fills our ears. This terrible grief is always the result of Herod's kind of way in the world. Trying to choose security and inviolability for ourselves seems to us to justify taking away the security and even the lives of others, one cycle of violence leading always to the next, until no one can even imagine any other way.

Although Matthew tells us that Herod's actions are the fulfilment of a prophecy in Jeremiah, that does not mean that Herod had no choice, or that God willed him to do what he did. But it does suggest that God knows and grieves over this response of ours. Deeply woven into the biblical picture of human nature is the knowledge that, endlessly, mindlessly, we choose security for ourselves at whatever cost to others. The story of Herod, like the stories we read day by day in the papers, suggests that this tactic simply never works.

But this is not God's way. God chooses to give himself and his security into our hands. He chooses to come close and still closer, giving and sharing, and never defending or retaliating. His way leads, admittedly, to the cross, but also to resurrection and life freely available for all. Perhaps his way would be worth a try.

The Second Sunday of Christmas

—— ∾ ——

Jeremiah 31.7–14
Ephesians 1.3–14
John 1.1–18

It is very difficult, in the middle of the school run or the super-
market shop, to remember that in us God is fulfilling the whole
purpose of creation. It is even more difficult to look at the news or
read the papers and believe that there even is a purpose to the world
at all, let alone that it is in the process of being fulfilled. But both
John and Ephesians assure us that it is.

God's purpose for his world is in-built from the moment of
creation. We are created through our redeemer and redeemed by
our creator. God in Christ is our source and our destiny. As the
Father creates us in the image of the Son, through the agency of the
Son and the Spirit, already the purpose is born that through them
we will be recreated, so that we can share in the true life for which
we were made, the life of God.

In Ephesians, the joy feels very close. Our inheritance is already
ours (Ephesians 1.11), not something far off that we long for, but
something that we already possess and can spend. Although we are
still awed by God's generosity, and amazed that he should have
chosen us, of all people, to share his joy, we can no longer doubt it,
because we have it in our hands. Although we can hardly believe
that God destined us – us! – to be a part of his family, even before
he made the world, with the Holy Spirit beside us, we cannot doubt
it for long. There is no temptation to preen and get too big for our
boots, because we cannot fool ourselves that God chose us because
of what we are. The very fact that we were chosen long before our
birth, or even the birth of any of the most ancient of our relatives,
makes it clear that it is none of our doing. It is God alone who gives
this unearned, unimaginable joy.

It is vital to remember that, and to share what we are given by
God, rather than hug it to ourselves with a sense of our own worth
and superiority. Jeremiah has seen his people so take their own

worth for granted that they hardly bother to think of God at all. God never forgets them or abandons them, they never cease to be his people, but they get complacent, and hardly care what their role in God's great work of creation is to be. They just want the land and the glory. They will get it, Jeremiah assures them, because it is what God has promised, and God does not break his promise. But the people Jeremiah sees pouring into Israel are not a mighty and triumphant horde, but a broken, tearful, hobbling mass, who can hardly believe what is happening to them. The remnant of the once proud people have long given up believing that they deserve to inherit God's promise. They are overwhelmed with gratitude and joy when they realize that God has never given up on them. As they limp and hobble home, helping each other along, they weep with amazed gladness. As God leads them in safety and comfort into his promises, they remember that God has always been their Father, only they didn't think, before, that they needed one. Now they know that they do. They thought that they could manage the world by themselves, but now they know that they can't: only God is their protector and their life. Now the joy that they feel is not vain and self-congratulatory, but full of awe and gratitude.

Jeremiah's rescued people and the Ephesians could join hands across the centuries and describe the experience they have in common. They know themselves to be vital to God and loved beyond anything they ever expected. But they also know that this is nothing to do with them. They have not deserved it in any way. It is one of God's inexplicable peculiarities that he has chosen them to be witnesses to his purposes for the world. They are allowed to feel the joy, always, but at all costs they must avoid complacency. Now that they know what God is like and what he plans for the world, they – and we – have a job to do. It is a job very like John the Baptist's. We are not the light, but we know who is.

Of course, it is possible to reject our role in God's purposes, but that will simply be our own loss. It is God's world and it will be what he has designed it to be, whether we join in or opt out. But when you hear about the joy of the Ephesians and the people of Jeremiah, why miss out?

Epiphany

The Epiphany

———— ❧ ————

Isaiah 60.1–6
Ephesians 3.1–12
Matthew 2.1–12

What strange people God chooses to be witnesses and messengers of his coming! They hardly seem the best way to announce to the world that its salvation is at hand. For example, this letter to the Ephesians – whether written by Paul or not – explicitly admits that the great missionary is in prison. How is he going to get on with his work there? Surely the Ephesians might be forgiven for taking him with a pinch of salt, when he writes about the great commission that has been given to him. He sits there in chains, and has the nerve to tell them that something is being revealed through him that has never been known before. The great prophets and men of God of all the preceding ages failed to notice this thing, and yet it is central to the whole plan of God. Do the Ephesians snigger behind their hands and say, 'If God tells him secrets, how come he didn't know enough to avoid being captured?'

Perhaps the Ephesians have more understanding than many. After all, the letter suggests that they have already accepted the gospel of Jesus Christ, and have at least heard of the Apostle Paul and his work, even if they have never met him. What's more, many of them have already been directly affected by this great secret that God has been revealing through the work of Paul. The secret is that God chooses all people to know him and share his mission, not just one race, as used to be claimed. Many of the Ephesians know that they would not be Christians if God had not revealed to Paul that Gentiles, too, were to be included.

But if the Ephesians are prepared to believe that step, what about the next? Next it is claimed that the Christian Church, now that it includes Gentiles as well as Jews, can be used to show the world the 'wisdom of God' (Ephesians 3.10). At that point, even if the Ephesians don't laugh out loud, some of us might be tempted to. We have got rather more used to thinking of the Church as a kind of tolerated, slightly senile old relative. We wouldn't dream of getting rid of it, but we really can't expect much from it.

Ephesians, on the other hand, thinks of the Church as a major player in the cosmos. Before the coming of the Church, the 'rulers and authorities in the heavenly places' (Ephesians 3.10) managed to gain control and status for themselves, and persuade themselves and many others that they, not God, were in charge of the destiny of the world. But now the Church, with its intimate knowledge of the mind of God, can challenge these other powers. Ephesians sees the Church as God's secret weapon in the struggle to bring the world to freedom and to worship of the true God.

But if, looking round at the congregations that we know and love, that seems like a ludicrous assumption, it may be that we have, ourselves, been taken in by the other 'rulers and authorities'. It may be that they have persuaded us to accept their definition of power and success. But we, the Church, are created with an entirely different set of assumptions and priorities, and we must not let ourselves be tempted.

That's why it is quite right and proper that Paul witnesses in chains to this stupendous calling. That is why the passage emphasizes Paul's humility. This great secret was not revealed to him because he was clever, and because he alone was prepared to understand what God had been trying to say for ages. On the contrary, he knows that he is the 'very least of all the saints' (Ephesians 3.8), and that his story starts with wilful misunderstanding and even persecution of God's Church. What fits him to be a carrier of God's secret is his knowledge of his own inadequacy and dependence upon God.

Perhaps the wise men started off with other ideas. Perhaps they believed that it was their wisdom and observational accuracy that allowed them alone to chart the rising of the star and follow it. They certainly believed that the sign they were witnessing was the stuff for kings, which is why they called on Herod. Possibly they expected to be rewarded and to play a large part in this new reign they had come to announce. But at last, at last, they come to the stable and the child. Whatever their previous misconceptions, like Paul, they recognize Christ when they meet him. As they rise from the floor and make their joyful way out of the story, they have helped to witness, yet again, to the way in which God plans to free the universe and bring it into union with himself.

The First Sunday of Epiphany

—— ∼ ——

Isaiah 42.1–9
Acts 10.34–43
Matthew 3.13–17

Matthew's is the only Gospel that shows any embarrassment about Jesus's baptism by John the Baptist. In all of the Gospels, John knows that his baptism is a temporary measure, but he also knows that it is a necessary one, and that his own message of repentance through baptism is part of the build-up to the coming of the Messiah. John's Gospel, which, typically, does not directly refer to Jesus being baptized, though it undoubtedly knows about it, shows John recognizing Jesus at once as the fulfilment of his work. It is what John has been destined to do since the beginning of time, as the magnificent opening verses of the Gospel make clear. Luke and Mark give the Baptist a less pivotal role. In both of these Gospels, it is possible to read God's affirmation of Jesus and his mission as something heard and seen by Jesus alone. But none of these three Gospels is worried about the fact that John exhorts people to come to baptism to be washed clean of their sins.

But in Matthew, we have some conversation between Jesus and John, which places John's witness at the heart of the event. John knows that Jesus does not need to repent and be made clean, and he tries to reverse their roles and get Jesus to baptize him, rather than vice versa. So when Jesus insists, John too, presumably, hears the words of the Father, as confirmation not only of Jesus's own calling, but also of the completion of John's. Jesus's acceptance of this unnecessary baptism marks the end of an era. He takes on baptism 'for now' (Matthew 3.15) because until the voice of the Father initiates the new age, we are still in the period of the forerunner. It is John's task to carry the baton to this point, and Jesus accepts it. From the moment he comes out of the water, however, everything changes. John's baptism becomes obsolete. A new baptism is to mark the new age – baptism into the Son, through the Holy Spirit. But even this will not start while Jesus is physically

22

present. Jesus and his followers do not baptize during Jesus's earthly ministry, because they need no other symbol of unity with God. They are walking and talking with the source of all symbols.

This slight display of uneasiness about the baptism on Matthew's part is intriguing, though it is equally interesting that the other Gospels don't feel it at all. But all of them are clear that this marks a turning-point. From now on, the hidden years of Jesus's childhood and youth are over, and he steps out on to the public stage. His birth into the human condition is his first public act of obedience to the Father, although it is witnessed and understood only by a few. Presumably the human mind of the tiny child could only be implicitly involved in that act of obedience. But here at baptism Jesus submits himself to his calling. He may not know exactly what it will involve, but he knows it is the will of the Father, and he knows that it is symbolized by this act of solidarity with the state of all humanity. If, in the world that we have made for ourselves to live in, we need to repent and be cleansed from our sins, then that is the world that Jesus, in obedience to the Father, chooses too. He chooses to be like us, and his choice brings forth the Father's words of love and approval.

So now he knows, if he ever doubted it, that this is the path he is to walk. It is one of identification, not of superiority. It will involve the painful truths of being human, not to be avoided but to be embraced. And through his embrace of the symbol of baptism, Jesus wrenches all the polite fictions away from it and reveals it for what it is. This is not a superficial matter of washing away a little dirt. This is about sin, which leads to our death. As Jesus steps into the water, he accepts the cross, too, because they go together.

After Jesus's death and resurrection, we accept that too. Christian baptism is an acceptance of death, the death of all the things that create a world that is separate from God. Jesus receives our baptism and death so that we can receive his resurrection and life. He shares our reality so that we can share his. It may be hard and painful to let go of the approximation of reality that we thought was the world, but as we step down into the waters, we hear the voice of Truth, calling us beloved and pleasing.

The Second Sunday of Epiphany

—— ∾ ——

Isaiah 49.1–7
1 Corinthians 1.1–9
John 1.29–42

To be called by God is a thing of joy and terror, in about equal measures. The Corinthians are largely experiencing the excitement, at present, but their walk of discipleship will certainly lead them to sympathize, at times, with the prophet who speaks in Isaiah 49.

The prophet speaks of his calling as something about which he had no choice. Like Jeremiah (see Jeremiah 1.5), this prophet cannot remember a time when he was unaware that he had been called by God, and that that calling was the foundation of his whole being. Not that that was necessarily obvious to others. Indeed, he specifically says that God hides him away, at least for a while. He doesn't say why – perhaps he didn't know. Another recurrent theme in the lives of those called by God is learning to live with both knowledge and ignorance. They are shown into the workings of God's plan just as far as they need to be to fulfil their task and no further. They can never deceive themselves that they are co-designers of the plan. They simply announce what they have been told.

There is obviously some frustration involved in this annoying way of working. Because the prophet – and any other servant of God – does not know all the details of how things should be going, it is quite impossible to tell whether or not he is succeeding in his task. Most of the time, he is sure that he can't be, because there are no visible results at all.

But just as the prophet turns to God and says, 'I'm really sorry. I did my best, but I've failed. You know how hard I tried. I'm very sorry', at this point of despair, God suddenly reveals that the task is much bigger than the prophet ever dreamed. He thought he was being sent to his own people, Israel, but God says to him, 'Not just Israel, but the world.' It doesn't seem the best possible management practice to tell an employee who is already discouraged that actually his job is to get much harder.

24

But it is thanks to the prophet, and many others before and after him, who began to glimpse the enormity of God's salvation, that the Corinthians – and we – are part of the story at all. The Corinthians are not yet aware that God's personnel practices are strange, and that knowing your weakness is often the qualification that God chiefly looks for in his followers. But Paul is going to do his best to tell them. He starts cautiously, with well-judged praise. But even that is laced with phrases that should make the Corinthians pause. Paul tells them that they are called to be saints – but so are thousands of others who call on the name of Jesus. The Corinthians might have thought that they were special, but they are not. Anyone who calls on Jesus is the equal of the sophisticated and intellectual Corinthian believers. Paul acknowledges that they are, indeed, a very impressive bunch. They are doing brilliantly in their public witness, at least when it involves exciting speeches. Is there a hint that their lives are perhaps not quite such good missionary material (see 1 Corinthians 1.8)? The whole of the correspondence between Paul and the Corinthian church suggests that these are exuberant, confident Christians, who are slightly inclined to put their trust in themselves and in the outward signs of Christian power, rather than in God, or in each other.

One of the big changes between the prophet who speaks in Isaiah and the Corinthian Christians is the number of people who share in God's calling. The prophet experiences loneliness and misunderstanding, and his task is often a solitary one. But Christians are called to be witnesses together, and to learn from each other as well as from God. The thing that we are most apt to underrate or even despise – the Church – is the thing that the prophets would most have envied. So the first thing we see Jesus doing, as he emerges from the waters of baptism, is calling a group of people together. They have no idea how much they are to go through together, and how much they will need each other, or how much they will accomplish, and how their names will be revered down the centuries.

John the Baptist affirms that Jesus lives and moves in the power of God. And Jesus, the beloved Son, feeling the presence of the Holy Spirit, instantly begins to build a community that will be able to hold that knowledge for the world, and share it. Like Jesus, and thanks to Jesus, we too are beloved children of God, full of his Holy Spirit, called to share God's love with the world.

The Third Sunday of Epiphany

—— ∼ ——

Isaiah 9.1–4
1 Corinthians 1.10–18
Matthew 4.12–23

Corinth in the first century was a busy, loud, exciting place. It had been a reasonably wealthy trading centre for a couple of centuries at least, and that had attracted people of many religions and races to settle there. The Jewish writer Philo tells us that there was a flourishing Jewish community in Corinth, and other classical writers detail temples to gods and goddesses of the Greek pantheon, possibly including Aphrodite. In other words, to be a Corinthian was to have grown up in a diverse, competitive, multicultural society. When Christian missionaries came to Corinth, they obviously found it difficult to change this basic ethos.

Acts 18 gives us one account of Paul's own missionary activity in Corinth, which clearly had its ups and downs, but was also highly successful. It also tells us, intriguingly, that Paul stayed in Corinth for eighteen months, which is quite a long time in his whirlwind career, suggesting that Paul not only saw enormous opportunities for the gospel, but also that he grew rather fond of the place. Certainly, in Acts and in the Corinthian correspondence itself, a lot of people are mentioned by name, so Paul not only kept in close touch with his converts, but also expected them to be known to the wider Christian community as people of substance.

But Paul was not the only one to see the potential in Corinth. Other missionaries, too, preached there. It is hard to tell if there was a spirit of rivalry among the different missionaries themselves, or whether this is just typical of Corinthians to pick up a good idea and turn it into something to argue about, but either way, the outcome is certainly a divided and contentious church.

Paul is not afraid of a bit of Christian infighting when he believes the truth is at stake – you might like to check out Galatians 2.11–14, to see Paul naming names in a big way when his mission to preach to the Gentiles is under threat. But here in Corinth, he is clear that the gospel is not just being undermined but is actually being fundamentally misunderstood because the Christian community is divided. Corinthian Christians are being fiercely loyal to whichever one of the missionaries it was that brought the gospel to their own particular group, and they are forgetting what the gospel is actually about. Whose death brought you salvation, Paul demands? In whose name do you accept the baptism that leads to new life? Is this about your teacher, or your God?

Paul knows very well that the gospel of Christ is rubbing against the grain, not just for Corinthians, but for most of us. The competitive instinct, the instinct to dominate, the instinct to define our own value by denying somebody else's is so basic, that Paul knows the gospel sounds like 'foolishness' to most of us, most of the time. As the Corinthians – and we – fight about who has the 'best' version of the gospel, they are turning their backs on the crucified God. What has the cross to do with the aggressive determination to be proved right? But it is the cross that is God's way in the world, and the demonstration of his power. The power to accept, create, recreate and save is so stunningly different from anything we understand as power that it is barely recognizable.

When Jesus walks beside the Sea of Galilee, what is it about him that the fishermen see? He is quite alone, as far as we can see. They do not know the stories of his birth, of how the mysterious travellers were taught a lesson about kingship. As far as Matthew knows, they were not present when the heavens opened and God proclaimed his love for his Son at Jordan. They do not know what Jesus has just been through in the wilderness, as he discovers what he must reject. All of this we, the readers, have just seen in Matthew's first four chapters. But Peter, Andrew, James and John come to it new, without the benefit of all these huge hints, and yet they drop their nets to follow Jesus. Jesus doesn't even offer them any very obvious inducements. There is no mention of fame, fortune, success, excitement. Instead, he offers them a mission, a chance to attract others, as they have just been attracted. Their acceptance starts the chain reaction that has never quite fizzled out, despite many wrong turns and shameful misunderstandings. We continue to preach the puzzling, spectacular, strange, unearned foolishness of God, who loves us and saves us. Christians have been as guilty as anyone else of wanting to be clever, successful and right, but if we keep preaching Christ crucified, maybe one day we will convert even ourselves.

The Fourth Sunday of Epiphany

—— ❧ ——

1 Kings 17.8–16
1 Corinthians 1.18–31
John 2.1–11

Most of us think we would like the kind of communication with God that Elijah has. The narrator of 1 Kings tells us, very matter-of-factly, that God tells Elijah to do something, and Elijah goes off and does it. And, in return, God makes special provision for Elijah, to ensure that he is protected from the results of what he has to say on behalf of God. Immediately before the passage set for today, Elijah has gone to King Ahab and told him that the Lord has decreed that there will be a terrible drought. Then, as the land and its inhabitants begin to suffer, Elijah is given instructions by God, taking him first to one place and then to another where he will be able to find water.

How lovely, we think, to know exactly what God wants from us! If only God would be as clear in his directions to us, how we would love to be as obedient as Elijah! But if you look a little more closely at Elijah's life, I suspect you will find that you don't mean it. To go to the King and tell him that his land is about to suffer a human and economic tragedy, with the implication that this is the King's fault, because of his sinful lifestyle, is not an easy thing to do. And the relationship between Elijah and Ahab is not going to get any easier as the story unfolds over the next few chapters of 1 Kings. And then notice the fact that Elijah seems to have no home, and no friends. When the Lord says 'Jump', Elijah jumps, and that is not conducive to a happy and settled family life. What's more, although we know, and Elijah knew, that his message was from God, others around Elijah often doubted it. Elijah's calling is to solitude and uncertainty, and it requires enormous courage.

In today's passage, God tells Elijah that he has 'commanded a widow to feed you'. But when the widow actually comes on the scene, it is obvious that she has not heard the command, and is in total ignorance of her part. Nor has God actually yet given her anything with which she could feed Elijah. As always, it is Elijah who has to put into words what is to happen.

We are not told what the widow feels about it, when she does as Elijah tells her. It is hard to imagine that she is really enthusiastic about believing a total stranger to the point of giving him her last morsel. But the widow is almost as alone as Elijah, and much less powerful. She has few hopes or expectations for herself and her son, even before the drought comes and devastates the land. She is clearly in no position to argue, and you can hear her thinking to herself, 'Well, we are going to die anyway, so we may as well die with an empty stomach as a full one.' So she feeds Elijah, as the Lord had said she would, and thereby saves her household.

In one obvious sense, this story of God's miraculous provision clearly goes with today's Gospel reading about the exuberant production of wine for the wedding at Cana. Both are about God's care and generosity. But actually it goes even better with Paul's puzzling passage about the foolishness of God. Why is it only Elijah who can speak God's message to King Ahab? Why does God use the poor, desperate widow to nurture and be nurtured by his servant? With the power to supply endless provisions, Elijah would have been welcome anywhere, and could have picked a much cosier place to stay. Why does God choose the Corinthians, fractious, not very bright, of little social standing – a microcosm of what the Christian Church has always been, and still is? Why does he choose to come to us, as another human being, and suffer and die? As Paul points out, it just doesn't make sense, when you consider all the other options that God must have.

But what Paul is arguing is that it is absolutely vital to remember, all the time, that we do not understand God. God is, by definition, completely outside human possibilities. The minute we forget that, we are not talking about God any more. So ignorance and stupidity are basic to our calling – luckily for us! In us, as in the Corinthians, it is clear that 'wisdom, righteousness, sanctification and redemption' are not things we could manage for ourselves, so we know for sure that they are gifts from God. Knowing that, without God, we can hardly even be said to exist, that's the mark of the Christian, Paul tells us.

Ordinary Time

Proper 1

—— ≈ ——

Isaiah 58.1–12
1 Corinthians 2.1–16
Matthew 5.13–20

God is about to give you a present. You are very excited about this because, after all, a present from God is likely to be a particularly fine one. You also hope that God has been listening to the large hints you have been dropping. This present might at last be that thing you have been longing for. You unwrap it with shaking fingers, but when the paper falls away, you look at the object inside the parcel. You have no idea at all what it is. None of your friends has one. You have never seen anything like it.

Paul is saying that the Christian gospel is a bit like this. We think it is going to be something magnificent, something we have been longing for all our lives, but when we get it, we don't understand it at all.

What is it that we hope for and think we are getting from God? We are not completely stupid. We know it will be something 'religious'. Perhaps we hope for a sense of being at peace with ourselves. Perhaps we long to know that God is on our side. Perhaps we want the security and protection that the maker of the universe must surely be able to bestow on us. Perhaps, moving down the scale a bit, we want people to believe that we are good and religious, so God becomes a sort of status symbol for us. Perhaps we want to be part of a religious system that is clearly more powerful than any other and can put other people in their proper, subservient place. Most of us come to God with a mixture of these motives, and they are not all wholly bad. But they are all about us, and not about God.

The people to whom Isaiah writes might feel most indignant at his round condemnation of their religious practices. Here he is saying that the people seek God and delight in him, and that they strictly observe all the fast days, and wear sackcloth and lie down in the ashes out of their respect for God, and yet he says they are not acceptable to God. Whatever else can God possibly be expecting from them?

According to Isaiah, the answer is that God expects us to begin to see the world through his eyes, whereas we were rather hoping that he might see it through ours. In God's eyes, our little religious observances are like a kind of playacting. However well we do it, we turn straight from the play back to our ordinary, non-religious lives, as though the two were quite separate. But God wants us to be heart-broken with love and longing for the world, as he is. Our disciplines of hunger or self-denial are chosen, and we can pick them up and put them down at will. But there are many who have no such choice. For them, poverty, hunger, instability are their daily lot. Our religious disciplines should remind us that we and they are all human, all utterly dependent for life itself upon the God in whose image we are created. When we end our fasting, it is so that we can go out and share what we have with others. Our destiny lies together, because we are all equally dear to God. We cannot allow ourselves to be satisfied with having just our own needs met.

That's why Jesus says that his disciples are to be the salt of the earth and the light of the world. Their faith is not just – or even primarily – about themselves, but about their participation in God's work in the world. This is the fulfilment of the law, according to Jesus. The law is essentially a corporate thing. It is designed to build a people whose life together reflects the nature of God and so makes it more credible to others.

What, then, is this mysterious and unrecognizable present that God gives us? It is a gift that allows us to put others before ourselves. It allows us to care for the world as God does, so that we are incomplete while others suffer. Paul has found out how the gift works. It enables him, a proud man, to come in weakness and failure, and to trust in God. It helps him to rejoice at the faith of others, even if he gets no credit for it. It allows him to see and preach the crucified Christ as the measure of wisdom in the world. This gift does very little for our own personal comfort or sense of self-importance, and it will be sneered at and misunderstood by all who do not possess it. But it is a present that interprets the whole world, once you have the knack of it.

Proper 2

— ∾ —

Deuteronomy 30.15–20
1 Corinthians 3.1–9
Matthew 5.21–37

This passage in Matthew decisively contradicts anyone who would
like to see Jesus as a kind of well-meaning hippy, preaching an 'all
you need is love' kind of gospel. It is terribly easy to assume that
Jesus was into kindness and forgiveness and not judging anyone
and letting everyone make their own path, and it was only later that
the nasty old Church tried to introduce a whole set of rules and
regulations. But, in that case, whatever is going on here in
Matthew? In every single case, Jesus takes the prohibitions of the
law and makes them even harder to obey.

The passage set for today covers murder, adultery, divorce and
swearing, and it makes every one of us liable to extreme judgement,
apparently. Jesus condemns not just the acts themselves but also the
attitude that makes the acts possible. Anger leads to murder and
lust leads to adultery, and Jesus seems to be suggesting that anger
and lust are as culpable as the offences they lead to. He advocates
the extreme measure of cutting out any part of the body that leads
to temptation. All in all, this passage sounds like a fanatical rant,
and it has been roundly ignored by almost all Christians ever since.
Have you ever heard it suggested that anger is a sin that should
debar people from ordination, for example? Yet in this passage,
Jesus says that to be angry with a fellow Christian makes us liable
for judgement.

This material is peculiar to Matthew – you might like to look at
Luke 6.20–end to see how Luke's equivalent differs. But that
doesn't mean that we can simply discount this hard and unsettling
passage as Matthew's own invention. For one thing, Matthew hints
at a context that we see again in some of Paul's writings. Are
Christians actually still bound by Jewish law, or does grace replace
it? All the Gospels are agreed that there were conflicts between
Jesus and the Jewish authorities over the interpretation of the

day-to-day regulations of the law. On food laws and sabbath laws, Jesus seems to have been rather lax, but on divorce and remarriage he seems to have been harsher than many of his rabbinic contemporaries. The earlier chapters of Acts reflect considerable confusion among his followers about whether or not they are still essentially a sub-division within Judaism, or not. Eventually, partly through Paul's pioneering missionary work, we have come to accept that although we will always have close family ties with Judaism, Christians do not have to be Jews too. But it would be a mistake to think that that conclusion was easily arrived at, and the confusion over the issue comes through Jesus's own teaching, as well as through later attempts to apply it in a situation of Gentile mission.

So here in Matthew, just before the passage set for today, Jesus says, 'Do not think that I have come to abolish the law or the prophets' (Matthew 5.17), suggesting that there were some who did think precisely that. And Paul's tortuous theology in Romans of how old and new covenants relate obviously led some of his readers to the same conclusion. 'Should we continue to sin in order that grace may abound?' someone seems to have asked him (see Romans 6.2). Some people have clearly heard Jesus's teaching, and the early Church's preaching of it, as liberation from all rules and laws. It doesn't matter what we do, because God loves us and forgives us. Rules and regulations are only for those blind fools who have not accepted Jesus as their personal Lord and saviour.

But what both Paul and Matthew are trying to suggest is that if you take that attitude, then you are still actually living in the same world as the world of the law. You are still living with the rules and regulations, even if you are reacting against them. Paul's image in 1 Corinthians is that of babies. Babies may throw their baby food about, but that doesn't mean that they are ready for solids. Similarly, Christians who spend all their time boasting about how the law doesn't apply to them simply demonstrate how much they still need it. They are still utterly preoccupied with what they are allowed to do and what they can get away with.

So perhaps the reading from Deuteronomy is actually the key to all three readings today. The commandments are given to Israel as a source of life, a source of knowledge of God, the life-giver. They teach God's people how to live in God's world. Deuteronomy assumes that after a while these laws will become second nature, so that we will be able to look only at their core and basis, which is our love for God and his for us.

Proper 3

—— ❧ ——

Leviticus 19.1–2, 9–18
1 Corinthians 3.10–11, 16–23
Matthew 5.38–48

The passages from Leviticus and Matthew today are linked by the idea that our lives together as a community are designed to reflect our God. Matthew says we are to be perfect, as our heavenly Father is perfect, and Leviticus says we must be holy, because God is holy. These sayings are not abstract, but belong in the context of practical advice about how we are to do this job of showing the world what our God is like. But, all the same, they are frightening in the responsibility they assign to us.

Leviticus 19 has a lot in common with the Ten Commandments, often spelling out the implications of each clause. Its prescriptions sound odd to us, in that there are challenging and inspiring commandments about how to treat the poor, mixed together with detailed instructions about how long after being offered a sacrifice may be eaten. The lectionary chooses to leave out these verses in Leviticus 19.5–8, but that does lead to a certain loss of flavour. As far as the authors of Leviticus are concerned, the whole lot belongs together. No detail of the lives of God's people is more or less important. The steady beat of the refrain 'I am the LORD' (vv. 4, 10, 12, 14, 16, 18 etc.) is the heartbeat that keeps the blood flowing through the whole life of the people. It is the same heartbeat for the poor and the rich, the great and the small, the blind and the deaf, so that to attack any member of the community is suicidal – it is like cutting a vein.

This is not a message that any of us instinctively likes. Whatever we may know in theory, in practice we simply cannot help acting as though our needs are more important than the needs of others, and so we keep introducing malfunctions into our system, our life together. In today's reading from Matthew, Jesus is trying to get his listeners to compare their behaviour with God's. God gives life to everything, irrespective of whether or not it responds to its maker.

God 'makes the sun rise on the evil and on the good' (Matthew 5.45), whether they acknowledge this as his action or not. This is God's perfection that we are called to imitate. God does not see things divided into pieces, but whole, perfect, and that is what we have to learn to do. God sees that everything, whether it knows it or not, cares about it or not, is actually alive with the same life, which is his own. He sees the intricate tracery of the veins, carrying his blood throughout the body from his steadily beating heart that is the life-source of all that is. We may think of ourselves as separate, independent beings, but if we were to be detached from God's blood supply, we would soon find out how incapable we are of functioning without him.

Leviticus advises a strong, just community where all know that they will be fairly treated and so have no need to be selfish and self-protecting. You do not need to fight for your rights if they are being freely offered to you. But history clearly shows that such an ideal society is constantly being subverted by those who want more than just their rights. Greed and fear and selfishness so dominate our imaginations that we can never really believe that we have all that we need. We are convinced that if we are made to share fairly with the poor and the hungry we will not have enough for ourselves, despite all the evidence to the contrary.

So what Jesus offers in the Sermon on the Mount is a much more radical alternative. Those of us who know that we are children of our heavenly Father, and that our rights are guaranteed by him, need to be foolishly generous to others. We have to allow ourselves, Jesus suggests, to be treated unfairly by the greedy and the powerful and the anxious, because we know that nothing they can do can actually dispossess us. So Matthew 5.38–42 is a vision of how the justified are to live in an unjust world. Don't fight it, humour it. Play with it, give it even more than it asks for. Perhaps at last it will think to ask about where your own security comes from, and how you can afford to be so madly generous. Then we might have a chance to share this vision of a world that is whole, connected together by the loving life of God, where to diminish another is to damage ourselves.

Christians are as tempted to dismemberment as anyone else, as the reading today from 1 Corinthians shows. Think about what unites you, not what separates, Paul urges.

The Second Sunday Before Lent

—— ∾ ——

Genesis 1.1–23
Romans 8.18–25
Matthew 6.25–34

Today's Gospel reading reminds us how important it is not simply to take all passages of Scripture and apply them directly to ourselves, as though they had no original context and no intervening history. Jesus tells his hearers that God will give them everything they need, if they only set their hearts on the kingdom of God, but many, many people have perished for lack of food, clothing and basic necessities. Are we to assume that they somehow failed to concentrate sufficiently on the Kingdom, and so were punished, whereas we, who have the good fortune to live comparatively sheltered lives, are also much better at keeping our hearts fixed on God? I think not.

Part of the discipline, then, of understanding what this text might mean is to try to imagine the people Jesus was speaking to. If you read the rest of the Sermon on the Mount (chapters 5—7), you begin to build up a picture of a fairly settled, law-abiding crowd. They are not so well off that they are cushioned from day-to-day worry entirely, but they have some savings and some education, and they are reasonably satisfied with their lives. Everything Jesus says to them is provocative and challenging to such a way of life, and with at least some part of themselves, they want to be provoked: otherwise what are they doing, following Jesus and listening to his teaching?

So instead of listening for the reassurance, we need to listen for the challenge – not what God promises, which this crowd already have, but what God asks. The radical, imaginative picture of discipleship that Jesus offers in the Sermon on the Mount is meant to shake us loose from the petty things and get us excited by the possibility of a new and adventurous attitude to life.

It is, perhaps, the kind of adventurousness that is found in God himself, in the first chapter of Genesis. This picture of God at work positively fizzes with excitement. The description is full of excess. As God talks – picture the three persons of the Trinity, shouting out to each other, 'Come and look at this!', 'Let's have another few hundred kinds of trees or animal. This is working so well!' – as God talks, roaming around in what is being made, colour and scent and noise spread out where once there had been nothing. And God just loves it. On any one of the 'days' of creation, he could have stopped, satisfied with what he had made, but instead he goes on and on, until at last he makes something that is as like himself as possible. And then what does he do, with all this glorious profusion he has made? He gives it away. He shares it with this, his final creature, because that is the whole point of it. The pleasure is not just for himself. A pleasure shared is a pleasure tripled – perhaps God the Trinity already knew that, long before creation.

In this image of God the creator, we see the essence of a joy that resists the worries and cares of tomorrow. In creating, God knows the risks he takes, and yet delights in what he has made. Up on the mountain, looking down at the puzzled and hopeful crowd, is Jesus trying to give them some sense of that kind of delight in life and creation?

Paul has certainly got the picture. It is an inspired idea to put Genesis 1 and Romans 8 together. Genesis lays out very clearly how things are meant to be, what joy each part of creation is meant to give the rest, and how all of it is there to love and be loved by the human creatures whom God makes to be sharers in his own pleasure. And in Romans we see the whole of the rest of creation waiting with agonized longing for human beings to catch up with the plot. 'How can they be so dense?' creation cries. 'Surely it is perfectly obvious?' 'Let's give them a few more clues,' suggests God. 'Let's show them some of the plot in advance.'

It is typical of Paul's realism to say that this knowledge, in the form of the presence of the Holy Spirit, is not there to make it easier for us. If God thought ease was the most important thing, he would hardly have risked creating. But the gift, the hint, the 'first fruits' of the Spirit do allow us to glimpse something of the glory of what God intends, it gives us that taste of the exhilaration of creation which might actually make us want to 'strive for the kingdom of God and his righteousness'.

The Sunday Next Before Lent

—— ∾ ——

Exodus 24.12–18
2 Peter 1.16–21
Matthew 17.1–9

What is the purpose of the transfiguration of Jesus? Is it supposed to reassure and confirm or baffle and alarm? And who is it for? Is it for Jesus himself, or for the disciples?

Matthew, like Luke, follows Mark in placing the transfiguration shortly after the disciples have admitted out loud that they believe Jesus to be the Messiah. So they have already made their decision about Jesus – it isn't prompted by what they see on the mountain. But if it is indeed God's confirmation of what they have already come to believe about Jesus, why are they not allowed to share it with anyone else? Peter, James and John are the only ones to have seen it, and they are specifically told that their news is embargoed until after the resurrection.

Certainly, by the time 2 Peter is being written, the apostles' eyewitness account is being used to give heart to a community that is beginning to doubt. They are beginning to suspect that they have been sold a line, no different from the stories that other cults put out. They had almost certainly converted to Christianity in the expectation that the world would soon end, and they would be on the winning side. But as the Second Coming delayed, so they began to wonder if they had backed the right horse, after all. In this context, the writer of the epistle is offering them the strongest possible proof that Christ is the one approved by God – he is offering them a witness, who speaks from his own experience.

In other words, in the context of this early Christian community, the witness to the events of the transfiguration is being used to back up what Christians already know of the nature and purpose of God. They know through the prophets and through the apostolic preaching of the gospel of Christ what kind of a God they are dealing with. Their temptation is to discouragement,

40

and so they need to hear again the words from God, 'This *is* my Son, my Beloved' – you *have* made the right choice.

But in the Gospel context that is not how God's words would be heard by the first disciples. They are already struggling with Jesus's interpretation of his own mission. When, in the chapter immediately before today's Gospel, Jesus tries to explain to them that they are right to call him Messiah, but wrong in all their expectations of what a Messiah should be, their incomprehension is painful. The fact that only Peter tries to argue by no means suggests that the others are convinced.

So when they come to the mountain of transfiguration, how are they likely to hear God's words? Is there any chance at all that they are going to hear them as God's seal on all that Jesus has said? Or are they going to hear the words of love and approval as an endorsement of their own interpretation? Might they not think, if God loves Jesus so much, he will certainly make him victorious? The temptation to assume that God is on their side, and to discount the fearful picture of the mission of the Messiah that Jesus has been trying to paint must have been enormous.

After the crucifixion and the resurrection, of course, the story can be told. The disciples are not then in danger of thinking that Jesus's Messiahship can be simply glorious. They have seen with their own eyes how God works, and the experience of the transfiguration can be put into its proper perspective by the reality of Jesus's death and rising to life. They can understand that God does indeed love and approve of everything that Jesus is and has done, and they can see the pattern that their own mission must take, and that it must follow the hard path to life, not the easy path to success.

We are not told by the Gospel writers how the words affected Jesus. The Gospel writers are always very reserved in attributing thoughts and emotions to the Lord. But perhaps it is permissible to think that at a time when Jesus is very much alone, misunderstood by his disciples, alienated from his family and his people, and facing the terrible prospect of what is to come, he does long to know that he is loved by his Father, and that his sense of calling to the suffering of the cross is shared and approved by God.

When the Israelites see Moses disappearing into the fiery smoke, and when the disciples fall in fear at the voice of God, they demonstrate the fact that the presence of God is only reassuring if you actually trust the God you are faced with.

Lent

The First Sunday of Lent

———— ❧ ————

Genesis 2.15–17; 3.1–7
Romans 5.12–19
Matthew 4.1–11

The devil, we are told, is the father of lies. Here, in the wilderness, or in Eden, what is on offer is nothing but lies.

Look at the cunning of the tempter. First of all, the really basic approach to a starving man: get yourself some bread. Notice that the devil does not offer to fetch the bread himself, or use his power to produce it – Jesus is to do all the work. And, after all, what harm can it do? It's just food. Jesus is intending to eat again sometime soon, why not now?

When that one fails, the devil moves on to something a little more subtle. All right, Jesus can manage without food for a bit longer, but what about love? All this time in the wilderness, Jesus has been pondering who he is and what he has to do, with God's words of love and affirmation at his baptism ringing in his ears. After all, says the devil, you already know that God loves you, that you are special to him, so you're not asking for a demonstration of anything new. God's already said the words, without any prompting from you. Why not a little action as well?

Finally, the devil moves on to power, and here I think he has misjudged his man, through arrogance and vexation. In this offer to Jesus, the devil is going on what he knows about human nature from all his previous dealings with people – they crave power. After all, it worked with Adam and Eve. They believed, with no other proof at all, that eating the apple would make them like God, and they believed it because that was what they wanted. They knew, with some part of themselves, that they were made to be like God, but they had this sneaking feeling that there was more to it than God was letting on to them. Surely just living in harmony with things and taking care of all that God had made couldn't be what it was really like to be God?

So when the devil offers Jesus all the kingdoms of the world and

44

their splendour, he doesn't expect to have to make good his word. Do the kingdoms of this world actually belong to the devil? Are they within his gift? Who knows. Who cares, thinks the devil. All the things that the devil has offered are illusions, but such clever illusions, based on near-reality. Because Jesus does have the power to turn stones into bread, and he does know that he is God's beloved Son, just as Adam and Eve know that they are made in the image of God. What the devil offers they already have, but in their anxiety Adam and Eve do not notice that. Jesus, however, is too focused on the reality of God to be taken in by such an illusion.

When the devil offers Jesus power in exchange for worship, he doesn't realize how much of his own deepest desire he has betrayed. He longs to be God or, at least, to have what he imagines God has, because the strange irony is that the devil is as taken in by his own illusions as are Adam and Eve. He has not apparently noticed that God is not like that. The devil lives in his own world of illusions, longing to be what he is not, hating what he sees as his own incompleteness, just as he persuades Adam and Eve to hate theirs. Only Jesus is content to be what he is, God's beloved and obedient Son.

In Romans, Paul is talking about the pervasive and destructive effect of living in a world of illusions, and how what breaks through the web of deceit, through the anxiety and determination to have what we deserve, no more and no less, is God's self-gift. There is nothing in the fantasy world about giving away your rights out of love. And so here, Paul says, the illusion of sin can end. It is as though suddenly, in a room full of mirrors, we come across someone real.

'There comes a moment', C. S. Lewis writes in *Miracles*, 'when the children who have been playing at burglars hush suddenly: was that a **real** footstep in the hall? There comes a moment when people who have been dabbling in religion ('Man's search for God') suddenly draw back. Supposing we really found Him? We never meant it to come to that! Worse still, supposing He found us?'[1]

Letting go of illusions is hard. But when God, the gracious, self-giving God, finds us, then by amazing and wonderful irony we find that we are what we have longed to be: precious and made in his image.

---

[1] C. S. Lewis, *Miracles*, Geoffrey Bles, 1948, pp. 113–14.

The Second Sunday of Lent

—— ∕∾ ——

Genesis 12.1–4a
Romans 4.1–5, 13–17
John 3.1–17

This passage from John's Gospel is one where we usually just concentrate on the edited highlights, like, for example, the wonderful statement about the freedom and power of the Holy Spirit, or verse 16, of course, 'God so loved the world . . .' But as you look in more detail at the whole encounter between Jesus and Nicodemus, it becomes more and more baffling. What exactly did Nicodemus come for, and why is Jesus teasing and testing him?

Nicodemus arrives, we are told, by night. So clearly he does not want his visit advertised. But, all the same, he is being quite brave. He is a 'leader of the Jews', and the conflict between Jesus and the religious leaders is already well under way. So Nicodemus comes to test the water. He has heard about the 'signs' Jesus has been performing, and he is impressed. What's more, he is impressed for the right reasons, not just because the signs are exciting, but because Nicodemus reads them for God's meaning and presence.

So here, you might think, is a chance for Jesus to carry his message into the heart of the Pharisees' camp. If he can get Nicodemus on his side, he will have inside influence. But this is not at all how Jesus is playing it. Instead, he starts the baffling conversation with Nicodemus about being born again. You can hear the irritation and frustration in Nicodemus's voice as he questions Jesus. This is not the treatment he was expecting. He thought that Jesus would be pleased and grateful for his interest, but instead Jesus seems to be mocking him. 'You're supposed to be a teacher of Israel, but you don't understand anything,' Jesus remarks. 'It would be better if you just started again, like a little child.'

Part of the problem is that Nicodemus arrives talking about 'signs'. The Gospels are very full of people who want Jesus to do 'signs', and John's Gospel has already, in the first couple of chapters, explored the bitter irony of the way in which we view 'signs'.

In the opening chapter, we see God's creative word going largely unrecognized in his own world, and then the stories of the calling of the first disciples, who believe and follow Jesus without the benefit of any 'signs'. Then there is the story of the 'sign' unwillingly performed – the wedding at Cana. Finally, immediately before poor Nicodemus walks in, the Pharisees have demanded a 'sign' from Jesus to justify his cleansing of the temple. And Jesus offers them the enigmatic sign of his own ministry. But no one can be bothered to try and interpret that sign. The only kinds of signs they care about are the miraculous healings that are such a strongly attested part of Jesus's ministry. But what are they supposed to be 'signs' of? Are the people really willing to look beyond the sign itself and try to work out what it might be pointing to? Or do they want the miracles as a quick fix, signalling, if you bother to think even this far, only that God will do as you want him to?

To be fair to Nicodemus, he has not come asking for a sign for himself. He has put some thought into the matter, and he has interpreted Jesus's actions as being connected, in some way, with the activity of God. So he has come by night to have his cake and eat it. He comes, rather smugly, offering approval and support to Jesus, but clearly not willing to jeopardize his position as a 'leader of the Jews' until he is clear which is the winning side.

The luxury of sitting on the sidelines and hedging your bets is not one that Jesus offers. Nicodemus thinks he is backing a potential winner without risking himself too much, but instead he is standing in the presence of his God. And he, a teacher of Israel, who thinks he knows enough about God to discern him at work in Jesus, does not know that he is seeing not a sign-worker, but God's own Son. Confronted with the Son, inexpensive goodwill really will not do.

Jesus is offering Nicodemus a chance to enter the real world, the one that God created through the Word. Suddenly, Jesus stops teasing, and spells it out. There is only one way to find out what God is like and what his purposes are for the world, and that is to commit yourself to the Son of Man, whose lifting up on the cross is to be the true sign of God's loving design. Nicodemus cannot go home pretending to be baffled by what Jesus has said. He has to decide.

The Third Sunday of Lent

—— ⁓ ——

Exodus 17.1–7
Romans 5.1–11
John 4.5–42

John is a masterly storyteller, and this story of Jesus and the woman at the well is one of his best. The Samaritan woman comes out of the page, cheeky, brave, vulnerable, and Jesus responds to her with warmth and humour, leading her skilfully into confidences, encouraging her to get beyond the superficial flirtatiousness that is obviously her natural conversational medium.

All through their talk, the woman is trying to keep Jesus at a distance and keep the talk between them jokey. She is good at the quick repartee, and to begin with, Jesus responds on that level. But everything he says has a serious point to it. The woman resists cleverly, turning the offer of the water of life into a joke, and swiftly engaging in theological argument when her own personal circumstances come into question. But Jesus will not let her get away with it. Every time she tries to turn the conversation away from the personal, Jesus forces it back. Finally, in desperation, she makes a faith statement: 'I know that the Messiah is coming.' But if she hopes that that will satisfy Jesus, she is sadly mistaken. Her belief in the coming of the Messiah is safe and impersonal; she doesn't expect it to have any immediate effect on her day-to-day life; it's something that belongs in a vague and unspecified future. Immediately, Jesus pounces. 'I am he.'

Now what is the woman to do? The moment she has been putting off all her life, the moment of truth about her faith, is now standing in front of her, demanding a response. So she runs away. She runs to get help, to find other people who will make the decision for her. 'He can't be the Messiah, can he?', she asks. Does she hope the answer will be yes or no? Either way, she has her moment of glory. For once in her life, she is the centre of respectful attention, and everyone is listening to her. It doesn't last long, as verse 42 makes brutally plain.

48

But what a very odd ending this is to the story. We know that through the woman's agency, many people come to faith in Christ, but we are not told if she did. Did her natural inclination to put off important decisions win, or was she convinced?

We presumably like to think that if we were faced, as she was, with Jesus in person, declaring 'I am the Messiah', we would not hesitate for an instant. We would not dither or postpone or offer Jesus a lukewarm reception. But there are an awful lot of warning stories in the Bible that suggest that dithering is one of the things we are best at.

The stories about the journey of Moses and his people through the desert are very full of dithering. Every so often, the people really make an effort, and manage to believe and trust long enough to take one huge step. Usually, it's only after all other avenues are closed to them, but even so, they did finally manage to follow Moses out of Egypt. God then performs a whole series of mighty acts to direct and protect his people, but their memories are notoriously short. After God has fed them regularly on manna, we now find them squabbling with Moses because they are thirsty. They seem to feel that their one great act of faith in following Moses out of Egypt is all that is necessary, and now Moses has to be responsible for everything else that is to happen to them.

Both the Israelites and the woman at the well are unwilling to believe what is put in front of them. It is almost as though the very ease of it makes it unreal. The Israelites cannot connect God's past actions for them with their present need. Every new challenge throws them into a panic, instead of reinforcing their understanding of their God – while the woman at the well cannot believe that her life is ever going to change, and that she is being offered salvation, just like that, in the course of a conversation. The very simplicity of it makes it enormous.

Paul has the clue. God's mercy is there, all around us, long before we even think to look. The hard part is not that we have to deserve it, because we don't. The hard part is just that we have to accept it. That's why John's ending to the story of the Samaritan woman is such a challenge – you decide the end. Did she allow the generous waves of God's grace to overwhelm her, or did she sit down in the desert and moan about being thirsty?

The Fourth Sunday of Lent

— ∾ —

1 Samuel 16.1–13
Ephesians 5.8–14
John 9.1–41

All the time we are called to try and find the difficult balance between faithfulness to God's known work in the past, and prophetic discernment of God's new work now. Faced with a completely new challenge, the hardest thing of all is to try to discern whether it is from God or not. When the challenge is past, and the new insights it brought are absorbed and become part of the 'tradition', it is hard to imagine the time when we were unsure. We look back, and we see that this new thing is absolutely in keeping with the character of the God we worship, as displayed in all his past interaction with us. How could we possibly have doubted it? But then the next new thing comes over the horizon, and we are left floundering again.

So it is easy to sympathize with Samuel. God used him to anoint Saul and support him in battle, to be committed to him, as God's way for his people. And so Samuel does what God asks. But when God then tells him to abandon Saul and anoint another in his place, Samuel cannot so quickly change his emotions. He grieves for Saul. And when, with a heavy heart, he sets out to do God's bidding, he is still, however unconsciously, looking for a direct replacement for Saul – another big, strong, handsome warrior, who will command the respect of the people. Only Samuel's prophetic gift from God enables him obediently to know David when at last he meets him.

But if we can sympathize with Samuel, can we also sympathize with the 'Jews' in today's Gospel reading? They – like most of us – don't have the advantage of direct prophetic communication from God, but they do have a profound, lifelong knowledge of the God of the Scriptures, the God of Moses. This God called his people to be holy, and to show his own character through their obedience. So the observance of the sabbath is not a detachable element, but a part of all they know of how to serve God.

Now, in retrospect it may seem clear to us that they had allowed the rules to take the place of a genuine seeking for God. They had assumed that it is enough to follow the law of Moses, and that no deeper confrontation with God is required. But it is easy to be wise after the event, and not easy to apply that wisdom to ourselves. What clues and hints did the 'Jews' have, that in Jesus God was making new, direct and personal claims upon their lives?

They are faced with a man who, they believe, was blind as a punishment for his sinfulness, and who has been healed on the sabbath. Is the healing itself enough of a sign of God's presence to counteract their fixed belief in what God does and does not want from his people? Over and over again, they question the man who was blind, and over and over again, doggedly, he tells his tale, though his exasperation increases throughout the story. He, at least, is in no doubt about what has happened and how to feel about it.

As a last resort, the 'Jews' try to direct the man's joy into more suitable channels. They have to accept that he was indeed blind, and now he can see, and that Jesus is somehow involved in this, but they try to make the man leave out Jesus and go straight to God with his thanks. But the man is not having it. To him it is clear that the two are connected. The power that healed him is the power of God, but the saliva and the hands that made the mud are Jesus's. 'What's the problem?' he demands.

The problem is not just that the 'Jews' cannot connect God's new work in Jesus with his previous work, but that they really don't want to. There is something about Jesus that they just long to escape from. They, Jesus, says grimly, are the blind ones, and their blindness, unlike the man's, is caused by sin, because it is their deliberate choice.

Ephesians is clear that trying 'to find out what is pleasing to the Lord' is the daily task of Christians. Everything must be laid out in the light of God, nothing must be taken for granted or left unexamined by that light. Even what we think we know about God must be brought constantly under that piercing scrutiny, because there is no other source of light, and no other possibility of recognizing the new acts of our unchanging God.

The Fifth Sunday of Lent

—— ❧ ——

Ezekiel 37.1–14
Romans 8.6–11
John 11.1–45

There is a story that St Francis once got up to preach, looked down at the hushed, expectant faces below him and said, 'God has not given me anything to say to you.' And with that, he blessed the people, and got down again. Faced with today's readings from Ezekiel and John, I wish I had the courage to do that. The story of the dry bones and the story of the raising of Lazarus are so brilliantly and powerfully told that commentary on them seems like gilding the lily.

So let's start with the slightly less emotionally charged reading from Romans, which actually provides a useful key to the other two. Life, Paul suggests, is a symptom, not a cause. You are not alive because you have life in you, but because you have the Spirit of God in you. A life that is directed away from God is, whether it knows it or not, no life at all. It is not just that it misses the point, but that it is actively 'hostile', Paul says, to the point. The whole purpose of creation is to mirror God's creativity and love. So to try to live as though there is no God is to destroy the very thing for which we exist, and to drive ourselves further and further away from the source of our life, which is God.

In the Gospel reading for today, death is clearly subject to Jesus. But if the point of the story is to demonstrate beyond all possible doubt who Jesus is, through his mastery of that last great enemy, death, it also demonstrates that death is not negligible or cost-free, even for God incarnate. Jesus orchestrates this great miracle meticulously. He does not rush to rescue his ill friend. He wants it clear beyond any possible doubt that Lazarus is dead so that when they see life emerging from the stench of putrefaction, the onlookers cannot deceive themselves that this was just someone reviving from a faint. And then when Martha comes out to meet Jesus, he gives

52

her an unambiguous statement of his power: 'I am the resurrection and the life', and Martha accepts it without hesitation.

But suddenly, what has seemed an unmoved, almost callous, opportunity to demonstrate his power changes and becomes charged with human emotion. As Jesus sees Mary and her comforters crying, the reality of what has happened hits him. Even though Jesus knows that he is the resurrection and the life, the tears and the loss affect him, and he weeps. This is one of those extraordinary moments when we see into the heart of the paradoxical things that Christianity says about God. Jesus is here to demonstrate God's absolute power of life over death, and yet he reacts as we all do to a life cut short, to the desolation of losing someone we love, and sharing the pain of others who mourn him, too.

And it is this Jesus, human, shaken, mourning, who goes to Lazarus's tomb and raises him from the dead. It is not an act of calm and majestic power, but an act of hope that love is stronger than death. Of course, after the resurrection, we know that to offer this hope is the purpose of the incarnation. We have chosen death, over and over again, as Paul reminds us, setting our hearts on our own needs as though their satisfaction could bring us life. But God offers us, in Jesus, a new way of being what we are meant to be, his children, made in his image. What we see in the raising of Lazarus is a foretaste of that hope that is offered to all through Jesus's own death and resurrection, the hope that God will not let us go out of the circle of his life and his love.

There is one more bit of irony in John's telling of this story. As Jesus goes out to demonstrate God's loving and life-giving power, he is, at the same time, setting the final seal on his own death. In going to Lazarus's home, Jesus is walking back into the full-blown hostility of 'the Jews'. Even as they sit, weeping professionally with Mary and Martha, they are waiting to see what Jesus will do. Will he risk coming back to visit his friend? How will he react to the death of someone he loves? Jesus's miracle and his words of liberation to Lazarus – 'Unbind him and let him go' – will lead directly to the decision to bring Jesus to his death. Lazarus's freedom and ours is bought by Jesus's imprisonment and death. We can only share in God's life because God is prepared to share in the death we chose for ourselves.

Palm Sunday

— ∿ —

Isaiah 50.4–9a
Philippians 2.5–11
Matthew 26.14—27.66

Betrayal.

At the surface level of the narrative, it is Jesus who is betrayed, over and over again, by friend and enemy alike. First there is Judas who suddenly, inexplicably, has had enough. As he sits eating with Jesus, he has already betrayed him in his heart and is looking for a way to make that betrayal real. Then there are the three disciples who go with Jesus to Gethsemane to pray with him in his agony of indecision. But despite the tense scene at supper, despite sharing the cup that Jesus explicitly tells them represents his blood, they seem unaware of what must follow, how much Jesus needs them. Their sleep betrays him. When they wake to find themselves surrounded by an angry mob, these three and the rest of the disciples run away.

Peter has, at least, a little more courage than the others. He does follow Jesus as he is dragged away. But as the night wears on, and it becomes clear that there is to be no rescue for Jesus, from heaven or earth, Peter betrays Jesus again.

For the Jewish authorities, the crowd of shouting, sneering onlookers and the bandits crucified with Jesus, the betrayal is at least not personal. They do not know Jesus as a friend and their leader. But they do willingly collude with Roman injustice, as Pilate does, caught up in the frenzy of hatred and excitement.

But if this is all about the betrayal of Jesus, it is also about self-betrayal. Pilate is supposed to be the authority-figure, the one who symbolizes order, the one who stands above the petty infighting of the local people. But even with his wife's words ringing in his ears, Pilate betrays everything on which his career has been based, and gives in to the chief priests and the crowd. How was he to know that this was to be his only claim to fame for the rest of time?

The religious authorities let themselves down doubly. They know Pilate despises them and cares nothing for their religion, and yet they are prepared to use his hated authority for their own ends. And in doing so, they betray their God, because they prove conclusively that they do not trust God to give judgement on Jesus. Instead, they make their own judgement and engineer his end accordingly.

Peter's self-betrayal is so enormous that he can never be the same person again. Peter, the impetuous, the outspoken, the brave. Peter who never hesitates but always leaps in with both feet first. Peter has been at the heart of Jesus's ministry from the beginning. He was one of the first to believe, one of the most vociferous in declaring Jesus to be the Messiah. He has seen Jesus teaching, preaching, healing. He is one of Jesus's closest friends, in the inner circle, one of the few who has seen the transfiguration and heard the voice of God acclaiming Jesus. Peter is absolutely confident that under no circumstances will he ever betray Jesus. All right, he made a mistake by going to sleep at the vital moment in the garden, but he didn't run away when the others did. He followed Jesus all the way into the heart of the enemy camp. What is happening to Peter in the hours that follow? Why does his confidence and love begin to seep away? What brings him to that moment of terrible desolation when the cock crows, and he knows what he has done? Whatever it is, it makes Peter the man to whom Jesus commits his people. Without that moment of stark betrayal, of knowing what he actually is at his most basic level, could Peter ever have been the rock on whom the Church was built? In the end, as he weeps, Peter knows that Jesus is more precious even than his own safety. He believes he has come to that discovery too late.

And what about Judas whose name is to become synonymous with betrayal? The Gospels give us no insight into Judas's motives, but they do tell us that, when it was done, he could not live with himself. Like Peter, when he sees the truth of himself in this betrayal, he cannot bear it. But if Peter goes back to his friends, those others who have also betrayed Jesus, and who must all face their lives with that knowledge, Judas's self-betrayal is even deeper. He will not accept the reality of himself. He would rather die. Could Judas's story have been any different? Peter the betrayer became Peter the rock, and Paul the persecutor became Paul the great missionary. Judas's greatest betrayal was in believing that God's grace and pardon were too small for his terrible sin.

Easter

Easter Sunday

— ∾ —

Jeremiah 31.1–6
Colossians 3.1–4
John 20.1–18

Real life is something so unusual that we can barely recognize it. Occasionally, we get a glimpse of it and it touches us with awe: the birth of a baby, for example, or listening to a perfectly performed piece of music, or a talk about the mathematics of infinity. All of these things have about them that combination of the ordinary and the completely mysterious that pings the chords of the mind and heart. In labour you know that what will come out will be a baby, but that tells you so little about the completely new character who is emerging. However much you may imagine what is growing inside you, or read all about the various stages of its development, or even see it, moving across the screen of the ultrasound scanner, the new-born child is still a complete surprise – utterly familiar and utterly strange.

The Gospel accounts of the risen Jesus suggest that when people encounter him, they do not immediately know him. On the whole, they are not terrified, they do not imagine themselves to be in the presence of an alien life-force, or anything like that. They recognize what is in front of them as a living human being, but not a familiar one. Even the people closest to him need help to connect the risen Jesus with the man they loved.

In today's reading from John's Gospel, you can, if you like, think of all kinds of reasons why Mary does not immediately see who Jesus is as he stands beside her in the garden. She is obviously in a terrible state, her eyes full of tears, and her imagination full of macabre visions of death and grave-robbers. She is utterly single-minded in her search for the dead body of her Lord, to the point where even a meeting with a pair of angels becomes uninteresting unless they can give her the one piece of information she wants.

But none of these seem real explanations of why she does not recognize Jesus. This is a woman whose whole mind is full of pictures of the man now standing beside her, and yet she does not know him. The simple explanation must be the true one – that real life is something we are poorly equipped to understand. So Jesus gives Mary the gift of sight, the gift of being able to connect the new life with the old. He says her name, and makes a bridge for her to see who he is, in all his extraordinary life.

By ourselves we do not have the power to see or understand God's vitality. By ourselves, we plod on, trying to be satisfied with the poor imitation that we call 'life', which is all about separation and death. But Jesus gives the gift of connection to the only true life, the life of the creator, which is about unity and sharing in the utterly real life of God. God's loving desire to share his life with us is implicit in everything he does, from creating us to redeeming us. Life is not 'natural' to us, but is a gift, reflecting the giver. Jeremiah puts into God's mouth the words 'I have loved you with an ever-lasting love, therefore I have continued my faithfulness to you' (v. 3), and that is the heart of it. We are loved into existence, and our continued existence is not our own doing but a demonstration of God's continuing commitment to us.

But for the moment we must be content with the sudden and fleeting reminders of God's eternal life that are available to us day by day. We have always before us the vision of the risen Christ, which helps us to recognize God's life where we see it. We have his voice, calling us by name so that, like Mary, we suddenly look up and see the Lord of life, standing beside us. And then, like Mary, we have to turn back to a world, utterly changed, yet devastatingly the same. We know this world now to be electric with the presence of God; we know our own lives now to be zinging with the resurrection life, and yet all of this is tantalizingly 'hidden with Christ in God' (Colossians 3.3). We are not called to cling to the presence of the risen Christ. Instead, like Mary, we are sent to shout out what we have seen. We are God's spies, now, searching for evidence of him in the robes of the gardener, listening for the familiar sound of the beloved voice of the Lord in the unrecognized strangers around us, helping to build the bridges of love that will enable others, too, to hear Jesus's voice and recognize the vast, free, unchanging, faithful love of God.

The Second Sunday of Easter

—— ❧ ——

Acts 2.14a, 22–32
1 Peter 1.3–9
John 20.19–31

What makes people believe? Probably the reasons are as numerous as the people who give them. Today's readings provide just a few examples.

In the Gospel, we have two sets of responses. First of all, there are the disciples, gathered together, their misery and fear locking them in far more effectively than the door that they think is doing the job. They have heard some rumours, from Mary and from Peter and the beloved disciple. But Mary is the only one who claims to have seen the Lord, and even she has to admit that she didn't recognize him at first. Would you believe under those circumstances? But then Jesus comes to them, unmistakably Jesus, full of extraordinary and unpredictable life, free to come and go as he pleases, but Jesus, all the same. And they believe.

But Thomas is still sceptical. He'll trust nobody's evidence but his own. Even his best friends can't convince him. 'Unless I see the mark of the nails in his hands and put my finger in the mark of the nails, and my hand in his side, I will not believe.' He lays out very precisely what will constitute proof, in his case. And Jesus gives it to him, uncannily echoing his exact words. Only now, Thomas does not need to do it, after all. What he needed was for Jesus to hear and respond, and Thomas believes.

In Acts, the process is more complicated. Peter is offering his audience a mixture of reasons for believing. First, he is offering them a new way of seeing what they already know to be true. They have heard about Jesus and about the signs and wonders that he performed, and they know what happened to him. Now Peter shows them, through their own scriptures, that this man they thought dead is actually alive with the life of God. As evidence of this, Peter then offers them himself and the other disciples as eyewitnesses. 'Go on,' he urges, 'ask us anything you like.' But lastly, and powerfully, Peter offers them a way of acknowledging what they have done. '*You* crucified him', Peter tells them. No beating about the bush there. Who knows how many of the people listening to Peter were actually present at the crucifixion? But present or not, Peter has judged rightly in thinking that his listeners feel a sense of collective guilt. They know that they and their representatives invoked the ungodly power of Rome to carry out their dirty work, and that Jesus was killed for no good reason. Now they can confess, and hear that God's purpose was not deflected by their unfaithfulness. They can repent and believe.

Finally, in 1 Peter readers are offered two reasons for believing: hope and community. The hope is what brought them there in the first place, the wild, ridiculous hope that this talk of the resurrection of Jesus was true. Because if it is true, then perhaps there really is some point to this world, perhaps we are not born simply to suffer and to die, but are actually part of a dynamic movement towards the kingdom of God. And having accepted the hope, they have stepped into a community of others who have thrown caution to the wind and decided to live as though life matters. Together, they will hold on to their hope, whatever the opposition, and when one feels like giving up, the others will remind them why they are here.

So the reasons for believing are many and various, and all of them will, at various times, appear ridiculous to others, and even to ourselves. One man's proof is another man's sneer. But at the heart of all of these proofs stands the risen Jesus, breathing out his life-giving Spirit. Life begins to fill our lungs, as we breathe in, standing in his presence, inhaling the fragrance of God's own life. The longing that it might be true, the longing for more of that tantalizing scent of the life of God, is what Augustine described in the fourth century, as he speaks to God. 'You called me, you cried aloud to me, you broke my barrier of deafness. You shone upon me, your radiance enveloped me, you put my blindness to flight. You shed your fragrance about me; I drew breath and now I gasp for your sweet odour. I tasted you, and now I hunger and thirst for you. You touched me, and I am inflamed with love of your peace.'[1] God in his graciousness may well meet you at the point at which you think you need proof in order to believe, as he met Thomas. But then he will give you himself, and after that, you will need nothing more.

---

[1] Augustine, *Confessions*, Penguin Classics, 1961, Bk 10, ch. 27.

The Third Sunday of Easter

——— ❧ ———

Acts 2.14a, 36–41
1 Peter 1.17–23
Luke 24.13–35

In his poem, 'The Lake Isle of Innisfree',[1] W. B. Yeats pictures a man so consumed with longing for home that even in the middle of a busy street, all he hears is the sound of the lake, more real than the shadowy place where he is actually standing.

What he longs for is the home of his imagination, on the Isle of Innisfree, where he will live in simplicity and peace. The slow beat of the poem's last line lets us see the man, standing stock still as the traffic flows around him, hearing the sound of the water of his dreams. Yeats did not, of course, abandon his literary life to live as a peasant by the lake at Innisfree, but the yearning that he expressed for a true home for his 'deep heart's core' is one that the readers of 1 Peter could easily understand. They, too, are standing in an alien land, longing for home.

But if they do not yet sit beside the lake, they are at least surrounded by their new family. 1 Peter reminds them that although they are living in exile, they know whose children they are, and so they know what is required of them. They can call God 'Father', with unimaginable intimacy, and although they come from many backgrounds and have had to be rescued from 'futile ways', they now know where they are going. For some unfathomable and utterly humbling reason, God's great plan for the salvation of the world waited for them, the ragbag of scraps from goodness knows how many cultures, to be ready, so that they could come home. They are bound together by that disproportionate gift that has made them a family, where before they were strangers, and set them on their path home, together.

Exactly the same thing is happening to the people who respond

---

[1] W. B. Yeats, 'The Lake Isle of Innisfree', *The New Oxford Book of English Verse*, OUP, 1972.

to Peter's speech in Acts. They are being made into a new family, with their loyalties changed, and their faces set in a new direction. Like the readers of 1 Peter, they know what it has cost to bring them here. In fact, their sense of the price paid for them is even stronger, because they recognize their own complicity in the death of Jesus. But that recognition is the start of the new life, and God's response to their contrition is overwhelming. They are to receive a share in his life, through the gift of the Holy Spirit. All around them, near and far, stretching away on every side, streaming into the future come the crowds of those who will now be their family, on the journey home together.

The disciples on the road to Emmaus do not know that theirs is a journey home. What are they doing, walking down that road with slow, distracted steps, talking as they go? Are they running away from the strange events in Jerusalem? If so, they are not very logical, because as soon as the stranger starts asking questions, they betray themselves as disciples of the recently crucified Jesus. If they are afraid, shouldn't they keep their mouths shut? Their most over-whelming need, greater even than their need for security, or space, or whatever it is that set them off on the road to Emmaus, is the need to talk. They have to find some sense in what is going on. They have talked themselves round in circles, unable to get to any sensible conclusion, and so they turn eagerly to the stranger, and the words pour out. They are past caring about whether he is a safe confidant.

At first they are angry with him. What luxury it is to be angry with a stranger! They must have been so angry with each other over the past few days, since the crucifixion. The only way to bear the guilt they all feel is to make sure they know it is shared. But here is some stupid idiot who seems not to know of the cataclysmic tragedy that has overturned all their hopes. But soon their anger is forgotten as they return again to their search. What is going on? What can it mean? They have asked themselves over and over again. All their hopes of Jesus confounded, and with them, all they had come to believe about God and his purposes. And then these strange rumours about the body being missing, about angels, about life. Oh, what can it mean? They turn to the stranger, too perplexed to realize how silly this ought to have been. How could he possibly answer?

Into their turmoil the stranger, who is no stranger, speaks his words of rough and humorous revelation. And suddenly the road to Emmaus is the road home, after all.

The Fourth Sunday of Easter

— ∿ —

Acts 2.42–7
1 Peter 2.19–25
John 10.1–10

It is easy to telescope these verses from St John's Gospel with verses 11–18. The second parable is also about sheep, and it is much clearer and more vivid, beginning as it does with Jesus's statement, 'I am the good shepherd'. But the parable we have today is more enigmatic, and repays careful study in its own right.

Picture a group of sheep. They are safe in their pen, which they know well, and they are keeping an eye on the only way in and out – the gate. A variety of people have been coming to that gate, and the sheep are all a little wary. They like it best when the shepherd comes. They know the shepherd, and he knows each one of them. He takes them out to places where they can get good pasture and feed safely. When he comes to the gate, they can abandon their watchfulness and just get on with eating, knowing that the shepherd will take care of them.

But when other people come to the gate, the sheep are in a quandary. Their instinct is to go out when the gate is open, because that is what they have always done. But they remember times when someone who wasn't the shepherd came and led them out, and they couldn't find the pasture, and didn't recognize his whistle, and some of them got lost. Ewes remember being separated from their lambs, and they all remember that the flock that made it home was smaller, less secure, and when they huddled together at night, they were not so warm and cosy.

Some of the sheep are recommending that they don't go out of the gate at all. That way, they know that they will be safe. But the other sheep point out that they will also starve to death if they don't go out to pasture. Poor bewildered sheep.

Clearly, this parable is at least partly a riddle. John tells us that its first hearers didn't understand it, and that Jesus had to explain that the point of the parable is not the shepherd, but the gate. A

64

closed gate functions to keep the sheep safely shut in, but the open gate is what this story is primarily interested in. It is the open gate that allows the shepherd to come in and it is the open gate that leads to the life-giving pastures. The strangers who confuse the sheep and the thieves who come to kill and rob all help to point to the one sure end. Sheep are always at risk, and they have to learn to value something more than safety. That something is what Jesus is offering them. The climax of the story is not security but abundant life.

At first glance, it might seem that the epistle of Peter has regressed in its interpretation of the sheep/shepherd motif, and gone back to putting the emphasis on safety again. It seems to be a very deeply held desire in us to see God as a kind of safety device, despite all the evidence to the contrary. We long to see God as the gate that keeps all danger out, instead of the gate that we go through into lush and exciting pasture. Isn't Peter just pandering to this desire, when he tells his readers that they have returned 'to the shepherd and guardian of your souls' (v. 25)?

But the only way that that phrase can be taken as superficial reassurance is if you detach it from its context. Otherwise what it says is that our shepherd and guardian, whom we must trust and emulate in all our doings, is the crucified Christ. Our gateway to life is made up of the wood of the cross. So in Christ we are indeed offered security, but on such a huge scale that it is almost frightening. What God gives us in Christ is the certainty that we are forgiven people, free to come and go in God's great pasture. For us sheep that is sometimes rather more than we might want. We might prefer a small mouthful of grass and then a quick scurry back into our reassuringly dull sheepfold. But that is too meagre a gift for God to offer.

So to 'return to the shepherd and guardian of your souls' is to step through the gateway of Christ's cross into an entirely new world, where we are no longer sheep, easily satisfied with small securities, but children of God, free to come and go in God's world. With that freedom comes responsibility, and a willingness to abandon our day-to-day security, as Jesus did, in order to gain the total security of being and doing what we are made for.

The Fifth Sunday of Easter

———— ✑ ————

Acts 7.55–60
1 Peter 2.2–10
John 14.1–14

What are we Christians supposed to feel about the world we live in? All three of today's readings suggest that, at the very least, the world is not our home. Stephen dies as though death is irrelevant, with his eyes fixed on the heavenly vision; Peter's readers leave all their previous identity to be like newborn children in their new race; and Jesus holds out to the disciples the picture of his Father's roomy mansion, to which we are all invited. Is this world, then, just something to be endured until we can get to where we really want to be?

Peter's letter has a high theology of the people of God. Although there is, of course, some debate about the author and date of the letter, the consensus is that it is indeed primarily the work of the Apostle Peter, writing at an early stage of the life of the new Christian community. His audience is a diverse group of people, from a number of different races and faiths, and they are facing hard times. It is clear that they are, in fact, going to have to learn to live in this world for rather longer than they might have hoped. The expectation of the immediate return of Jesus to take believers to the kingdom of God is already fading and, to make matters worse, Christians in some areas are facing mob violence. What Peter is offering them is a vision of who they are, a vision of their value and status that will sustain them through what is to come.

New allegiance, new race, new family, new life – these are at the heart of Peter's theology of the people of God. Once they belonged nowhere and had no importance, but now they are God's own people, chosen, royal, holy (v. 9). When they stand together, this motley crew of unimportant people become a rich, magnificent temple, bearing witness to the grandeur of God. And at the heart of this temple is Jesus, the Cornerstone.

As Stephen looks up to heaven, feeling the hate and the stones

66

battering at him, he too sees Jesus, and Jesus is standing next to God, part of his glory.

So Jesus is the key, the one who mediates an understanding of how we are to live in this world. In today's Gospel, it is easy to laugh at Thomas's stupidity as he asks what should have been obvious, but actually, he is asking the basic religious questions – what is God like, and how do we get to him? And Jesus's answer is the basic Christian answer – 'God is like Jesus, and can only be reached through Jesus, through following and imitating him.' A simple and utterly annoying answer. No system is given, no sets of rules, no course of study, with diplomas at the end, but a commitment to a person, whose life, death and resurrection reveal the world's creator and saviour.

In all the time that Thomas has been a follower of Jesus, he has known that Jesus's mission is about God. Thomas and the others have not always, or even often, understood what exactly is going on, but they have grasped that Jesus has the power to 'show us the Father'. They have felt the authority of Jesus, the strange, compelling novelty of his message about God, that yet makes sense of everything they already knew and had heard about God. Very occasionally, they seem to take the next step and realize that God cannot be understood independently of the witness of Jesus. Now, Jesus makes that explicit. 'I am the way, the truth and the life. No one comes to the Father except through me.'

So if Jesus is the way we follow, how does that way lead us through the world? Peter and Acts make it clear that Jesus's way is bound to involve suffering, but they do not suggest that we should hate the world, or count it as essentially unreal. As Stephen dies, gazing at the glory of God, the figure he sees is undoubtedly a human one. The humanity of Jesus, the incarnate God, is not accidental to God's relation to the world, but essential. God the creator makes a world and gives himself to it, without reservation, even to death. Our commitment to the world should be no less full. The result of God's self-giving in Jesus is the knowledge that every part of what is made, even death, can respond to its creator and be transformed. Peter urges his readers to come and be built into a temple where God can be joyfully praised and faithfully served. If Jesus chose to do that in this world, we, his followers, should be content to follow.

The Sixth Sunday of Easter

———— ❧ ————

Acts 17.22–31
1 Peter 3.13–22
John 14.15–21

It is hard to tell if Paul's famous speech at the Areopagus is a triumph or a disaster of evangelism. He has done his preparation well – one of the basic rules of preaching. He has walked around the city and talked and listened and picked up on the concerns of the people to whom he is talking, and the kind of religious language they are used to. So he hasn't simply used a set speech, but is deliberately trying to tap into the world-view of his audience.

In the section before today's reading from Acts, we find Paul stuck in Athens, waiting for Silas and Timothy. Being Paul, he doesn't take a holiday, but immediately throws himself into the fray, arguing with anyone who will listen, in the synagogue and the market place. Clearly, this kind of argument is meat and drink to the Athenians, and Paul quickly gathers crowds who are more than happy to listen to and join in with religious debate. They liked nothing better than a new religion.

So when they invite him, politely and formally, to come and address them about his ideas, Paul starts cautiously, with compliments. He has noticed, he says, that they are a deeply religious people. The audience nod and preen themselves slightly. Indeed, Paul goes on, they seem to be prepared to worship almost anything, and put up altars to nothing in particular, just in case. The audience frown, wondering if that is still a compliment, or does it, in fact, contain a hint of criticism?

Throughout the speech, Paul does this subtle, sharp blending of flattery and criticism, first complimenting them on the array of altars they have set up, then telling them that altars are useless; or agreeing with them that all people share a common humanity and derive from God, and then telling them that they are not perfect, and will have to repent and be judged.

Paul is building towards his climax, which is the introduction of

Jesus. But the crowd are not ready for this. Paul has correctly identified their religious instincts. They like novelty, variety. They want to control God through the service they offer to him, and they think that is best done by keeping all their options open and performing sacrifices at as many altars as possible. They are aware that their lives are limited and transitory, and they seek to find their meaning by seeing themselves as part of the divine life. All of this Paul understands but ruthlessly confronts. Certainly, he tells them, your lives do have meaning. They will be seen, in their entirety, and judged by God in Jesus. But judgement was not what the Athenians were looking for. They wanted affirmation, not responsibility. In particular, they do not want to be judged by a God they can't buy with worship. They want to bind God to them with the power and scope of their religious service, but God is not to be bound, Paul reminds them: he is utterly free, and needs nothing. He does not need gifts, but is the ultimate source of all there is to give. So you cannot buy meaning and certainty by the rich variety of your religious observance.

So, having demolished their religious props, what is Paul offering instead? He is offering Jesus, the man appointed by God, and affirmed through the resurrection. He is asking them to swap their great profusion of ideas and hopes, all their sources of religious insurance, for faith in one man. He is telling them that there is no easy way, through religious observance, to security, but only a hard way, through repentance and an acceptance of limits. And he asks them to believe this because God has shown it to be the truth by raising Jesus from the dead.

But Paul gets no further. In fact, he doesn't even have time to introduce the name of Jesus. Just the mention of judgement and resurrection are enough. The crowd are bored and incredulous. What is it that so alienates them? Is it the very idea of resurrection that they find so incredible? Or is it the smallness and particularity of what Paul is offering them in exchange for their profusion of religious beliefs? What if another new and exciting religion comes along? Surely Paul doesn't expect them to stick with this gloomy religion even then?

To believe that God might focus all truth and meaning in one man, Jesus, is hard, but perhaps mostly because we, like the Athenians, like novelty more than commitment, like the idea of controlling God more than the idea of giving God control, like the idea of our lives having meaning, but not that the meaning is God's, not ours.

The Seventh Sunday of Easter

— ∾ —

Acts 1.6–14
1 Peter 4.12–14; 5.6–11
John 17.1–11

Poor disciples. What they have been through over the last few weeks! What wild swings of emotion they have had to deal with. First of all the horrors of Good Friday, with the anguish they felt for Jesus, the fear for themselves, the guilt over what they had done, the confusion about their future now that Jesus's mission had apparently failed. Then the beginnings of the rumours that Jesus was alive, with all the hope and terror and sheer perplexity of that. And then, at last, normality again, though a much more wonderful normality than ever before, with Jesus back among them, talking, teaching, making them feel at the centre of God's world, as he always did.

It is very unclear from the Gospels and from Paul's writings how long this period between the resurrection and the ascension was. The Church's liturgical year suggests just a few weeks. In Matthew, it looks very short, while Paul seems to extend it to include the appearance to him on the Damascus road. John's account is the most vivid, with the details of significant meetings and memorable meals. But for sheer poignancy, these first few verses of Acts are hard to beat. In verse 6, the disciples are clearly imagining that life will now go on like it used to in the old days, only better. Jesus seems willing to concentrate only on them, with no preaching, teaching or healing outsiders, and he listens to them and answers their questions without the impatience and teasing that so often marked their relationship before. They have forgotten all their doubts about his mission, the terrible doubts that the crucifixion caused, and they are back to believing that Jesus is going to take over Israel, and that they will be part of the new ruling party.

And then suddenly they find that he is not going to stay, and that he expects them to carry on without him. As they trudge back to Jerusalem, back to the upper room again, the flatness of the description in Acts is striking. We hear nothing of their emotions – no fear, no despair, no joy. They are all out of feelings. Tiredly, they get on with things, waiting for whatever it was that Jesus said he would send to help them, though they are not sure that they will know it when it arrives.

So, one minute they are the inner circle, waiting to hear about the plans for the kingdom of Israel and their vital part in the matter, and the next minute, they are a leaderless, purposeless group of people. Jesus has refused, categorically (v. 7), to tell them what is going on, but instead has left them a job to do, and a very daunting one at that. They have to be his witnesses, all over the world, apparently. This Holy Spirit had better be good, whatever it is, if it is going to get this emotionally drained bunch of waifs and strays going again.

But they have at least learned two things through what they have all been through. They have learned to stick together – whatever happens this time, they all want to witness it together – and they have learned to keep praying. If the crucifixion did not mean the end of all they had understood about God, then God's purposes have to be deeper, wider and stranger than anything they could imagine, and their only chance of not getting it hopelessly wrong again is to keep praying. Perhaps they themselves hardly realize the significance of those two lessons learned, but sticking together and praying are to become two of the defining characteristics of the new Christian community that Acts is going to tell us about.

In today's Gospel, prayer and community are equally obvious. Jesus's prayer for the disciples is that they 'may be one as we are one' (v. 11). Christian unity bears witness to our understanding of God's unifying, reconciling work in Christ, which is not something he just chooses to do, but which demonstrates his own nature. (And, after such a statement, do you have to ask what Christian disunity bears witness to?)

Jesus's prayer for the disciples underpins what we have already seen in Acts. Jesus knows that the disciples may feel left behind, bereft, after the ascension. 'I am no longer in the world,' he says, 'but they are.' So he asks for protection for them. But not protection from fear, or persecution (as the reading from 1 Peter makes clear), or any of the things we might feel we want to be protected from. He asks for protection for his followers 'so that they may be one', and in their unity, demonstrate the loving unity of God.

Day of Pentecost

—— ∽ ——

Numbers 11.24–30
Acts 2.1–21
John 20.19–23

It is typical of God's calling to us that on the day of Pentecost, instead of being allowed to dwell on what it feels like and means to have tongues of fire resting on you, the disciples have to go straight out and start preaching. The Acts account has got it just right. The description of the giving of the Holy Spirit is over in four verses, and the sermon takes most of the rest of the chapter. The first four verses are full of vivid detail – the wild wind rocking the whole house, the tongues of flame, and the strange speech – but we are not allowed to dwell on them. We don't even hear how the disciples got out of the house and into the crowd, but suddenly, that's where they are. And now that they have reached their destination, the narrative slows down, and there is time for dialogue, reaction, emotion. But not from the disciples. Instead, we are now focusing on the crowd, on their bewilderment, amazement, disbelief. 'What about the disciples?' you want to shout. 'Were they bewildered, amazed, disbelieving? Or were they filled with joy, certainty and power?' 'You don't need to know,' Acts tells us firmly.

And that makes it clear what the gift of the Holy Spirit to the Church is for. It is not designed to fill us with religious feelings, or give us unshakeable certainty, or impress others with our power, or even to form us into The Church, though it may have all those effects too. The gift is given primarily to allow the disciples, and us, to do what Jesus told us to, which is to be his witnesses 'in Jerusalem, in all Judea and Samaria, and to the ends of the earth' (Acts 1.8).

So when at last we hear directly from the disciples, it is Peter's voice, lifted in praise of God. He knows, with utter clarity, that what has happened to them is a sign of God's huge and faithful purpose. This is what God has always promised, through his prophets, and the point of it is our salvation. The verses that Peter

72

quotes from Joel could be frightening, with their talk of the 'last days', the sun darkened and the moon turned to blood, but Peter is here to tell the crowd that God's presence is opportunity, not terror, salvation, not condemnation.

Peter's excitement and joy bubble through this speech. The immediate effect on Peter of the gift of the Spirit has been to make him wildly generous. He longs to share what has now become clear to him. He looks on the crowd around him, and he knows he is now responsible for them. He must, he absolutely must, make it clear to them what God is offering through faith in Christ.

That same dynamic is at work in the verses from John's Gospel. The Spirit is given as the disciples take up Jesus's mission, and its immediate effect is to send them out to take responsibility for the world. Throughout John's Gospel, the way in which people react to Jesus signals whether they will accept or reject God's forgiveness offered through him. Now the same thing is to happen to the disciples. Their mission, too, is to do with forgiveness and judgement. It sounds rather as though Jesus is giving the disciples a blank cheque when he says they now have the power to forgive sins or retain sins. But remember to whom this charge is given, and in what circumstances. This is a group of people who have just betrayed and deserted their leader, and now they have locked themselves in an upstairs room, fearing for their own lives. When Jesus comes to them, he shows them the marks of the nails, not just so that they can be sure who he really is, but so that the tremendous mission he is about to entrust to them can be founded in the reality of who they are too. These disciples know how much they have been forgiven. They are not going to take the power over sin lightly. The Christian mission starts in the knowledge of our own need.

The temptation is to see the gift of the Spirit as something for insiders, to be jealously guarded and enjoyed. But instead we need to share in Moses's generosity of vision, and long for the Spirit to come down on all of God's people. It is with that longing that Peter preaches, a longing that all should share in the forgiveness and new life that God has given to us. We receive in awed gratitude, and share because we know that God has given us what we do not deserve. Should we be more grudging than God?

Ordinary Time

Trinity Sunday

———— ∾ ————

Isaiah 40.12–17, 27–31
1 Corinthians 13.11–13
Matthew 28.16–20

The people whom this second section of Isaiah is addressing are completely worn out. They have not even got the energy actively to reject God and seek other sources of comfort. Instead, they sit around and whine. Even the young are slumped wearily, unable to summon up enthusiasm for anything. They believe that they are utterly forgotten and of no value to anyone, particularly God, and this feeling of being despised and neglected fills them with terrible lethargy. If God doesn't care, why should they? To them, Second Isaiah offers a picture of a God of patience and diligence, who forgets nothing.

Underlying it all is Isaiah's insistence upon the utter freedom and omniscience of God. 'Who can claim to have taught God anything?' Isaiah demands. God didn't need to ask advice when he was making the world, and he doesn't need to be told what to do now. But although this could be read as a sweeping put-down for these depressed Israelites, it isn't. Instead, it is to be the source of their comfort and joy. Because the God who made the world, without help or guidance from any, is not a careless God, but one whose measurements are fiercely exact. You may not be able to measure every drop of water in the world, or weigh a mountain, but God can and has. Your very insignificance is, funnily enough, a reassurance. Although 'the nations are like a drop from a bucket' (v. 15), and nothing in the world can provide a sacrifice that is worthy of God, yet this majestic God is Israel's Lord, who cares for them, as he always has done. When they are too tired, bewildered and woebegone to find any way out of their plight, they can remember that their God is inexhaustible. They can remember, reach out and feel the potent, unending energy of God.

That God is both sovereign and free and at the same time utterly committed to us is at the heart of all the Bible tells us about God.

Ordinary Time

In creation, incarnation and Pentecost we see God at work, patiently, with infinite attention to detail, drawing us into his incomprehensible freedom and life. So when Matthew and Paul end their writings with references to the Trinity, they are not just paying lip-service to something they have inherited and feel they must mention, but are witnessing to the thing that motivates them, and that they believe can energize the hard-pressed and doubting congregations to whom they are writing.

What Paul wishes for the Corinthian Christians is about as comprehensive as you can get. He prays for them 'the grace of the Lord Jesus Christ, the love of God, and the communion of the Holy Spirit'. Such a familiar phrase, but with such far-reaching consequences. Jesus's grace allowed him to accept the will of the Father, and follow his way, even to death and the cross. God's love led him to create all that is, and to send his only Son to offer redemption and life to everything that is made. And the Holy Spirit offers to us the communion which is shared by Father, Son and Spirit, the absolute love and rejoicing of the life of God.

'The communion of the Holy Spirit' is a particularly baffling phrase, and one that it is easy to gloss over. Augustine, thinking deeply about the biblical writings about the Holy Spirit, called the Spirit 'the bond of love' between Father and Son. It is almost as though – unimaginable thought – Father and Son would be somehow separated without whatever it is that is represented by the Holy Spirit. So if we wish upon ourselves the 'communion' of the Holy Spirit, we are praying to be unified, as Father, Son and Spirit are unified. We do not pray to be made indistinguishable, but we do pray to be made inseparable, and to give and get meaning only in each other.

So when Paul writes to a divided and bickering church, this is what he wishes for them. They are to love the world as God, its creator, loves it. They are to give themselves wholly to God's will for the world, as God the Son did, and they are to find their true selves, their only real identity, in belonging together and together serving God, in the communion of the Holy Spirit.

Christian baptism in the name of Father, Son and Holy Spirit is very ancient. Matthew witnesses that the command to do this was given by Jesus himself. And if Christians do not always, conspicuously, demonstrate in our lives that we rejoice in the world and in each other as God does, Isaiah reminds us that, unlike us, God 'does not grow faint and weary'.

77

Proper 4

—— ❧ ——

Deuteronomy 11.18–21, 26–28
Romans 1.16, 17; 3.22b–31
Matthew 7.21–29

These are frightening words from Jesus in today's Gospel reading. He imagines a group of people who truly believe they are his followers and yet are mistaken. These people perform mighty acts in the name of Jesus, but Jesus has no idea who they are. The people he knows and recognizes are the ones who act on what they have heard from Jesus and, since this comes at the end of the Sermon on the Mount, presumably Jesus is implying that they must act on what he has just been saying. The people Jesus is rejecting are only interested in 'religious' activity. They prophesy, cast out demons and do works of power in Jesus's name (Matthew 7.22), but when Jesus talks about 'religious' observance in Matthew 6, the contrast between his advice and the practices of these imaginary evil followers is quite striking. Jesus tells his disciples that the reward of genuine religious observance is the approval of God, not the admiration of the general public. The rest of the Sermon on the Mount is not really about what most people would recognize as 'religion' at all. It is about how we should live with each other in the presence of God.

But, of course, the whole of the Old Testament assumes that that is the heart of religion. God makes for himself a people who are to be instantly recognizable because of the way they treat each other. Their cultic and liturgical practices will simply be an extension of that life directed towards God. So Deuteronomy envisages God's commandments as the air that his people breathe. The outward symbols, bound on hand and head, will simply reflect the reality of the inward person, completely formed by the words of God, and forming the next generation in the same way, quite naturally. Jesus's words are to be like that for the people. They are to be so fully part of us that all our acts, whether we think of them as 'religious' or not, will speak of the Lord we follow.

But both Deuteronomy and Matthew recognize that people have a choice and that they do not always choose to bind the words of God into their very being. Jesus describes a man who builds his house on the sand, only to have it fall in the first storm. Deuteronomy is rather blunter – to choose to live against God's commandments is to bring down a curse on yourself. It is vital to keep this choice before us. It is the choice Jesus set before everyone he met, according to the Gospels. But in today's Gospel reading, as in so many of the encounters Jesus has, the choice doesn't look as clear as Deuteronomy seems to suggest. Over and over again, Jesus meets people who believe that they have made the right choice. They believe themselves to be following God's commandments, and many of them think that, as a matter of fact, they are being rather more obedient than Jesus is himself. And now Jesus is saying that his own followers are just as likely to deceive themselves, and believe that they have chosen obedience when they haven't at all.

And that's why, Paul says, we are always stupid to rely on ourselves. Rely instead on Jesus, he urges. Left to ourselves, we never quite manage to choose obedience, even when we think we have. We always manage to fasten on something irrelevant and make it the heart of our religion. So God, in his righteous mercy, gives us Jesus. Jesus is obedient as none of us can be, and generous too. Instead of using his obedience to show us up, he uses it to free us from our feeble attempts to get it right alone. Now all we need to know is that Jesus is the fulfilment of all that the law is trying to do. Jesus shows us the nature of God, and he draws around him a community of people who try to do the same, in the way we live together. We still need to try to live out God's commandments, since they do genuinely reflect what God desires for his people. And we will still fail, as people always have. But now we know that this isn't primarily about us, about how good or bad we are. We are not the central characters in this story. But the central players, Father, Son and Holy Spirit, draw us into their play. We cannot ruin it and we cannot run it, but we can enjoy it and make it clearer for the other new actors who come to take part. Some find it hard that they cannot be the stars, but most of us are only too delighted to share their reflected glory.

Proper 5

—— ∿ ——

Hosea 5.15—6.6
Romans 4.13–25
Matthew 9.9–13, 18–26

'I knew the great Apostle Paul. Buy me a drink, and I'll tell you all about him. I used to act as his secretary, sometimes, which I knew, even then, was a great honour. Of course, I didn't realize quite how important he was going to be, but even in the early days, you could tell he was a man to watch. He had such energy, and he was always talking and thinking. It was quite hard to keep up with him when he was dictating. Sometimes I'm afraid I may have missed out a few words, or got a bit muddled. I hear now that his churches kept his letters, and read them out over and over again, and I do hope I didn't make it harder for them.

'I volunteered to help him, of course, because I'm quite proud of my writing, but also because, in a way, I owe my right to believe in the Lord Jesus to him. He fought hard for Gentiles like me to be included with the others, and he needn't have bothered about us because, after all, he was a Jew himself.

'I hoped I might get to know him better, working with him, but he was a hard man to know. I still don't understand, to this day, why he gave up his family and his own tradition to join the Christians. Going around with him, I heard lots of stories about Jesus. The ones I liked best were the ones where Jesus goes out of his way to help people that the respectable folk wouldn't touch with a bargepole. He used to eat with collaborators and prostitutes, so they say, and touch lepers and unclean women, and even I wouldn't want to do that, though I've had a varied life myself, and often been short of the next meal.

'It's easy to understand why people like that would want to follow Jesus. Or the people who came to him for healing, when everything else had failed. I heard a lovely story about how he cured a little girl when everyone else said she was dead. And her father was a leader of the synagogue, a respectable man, like Paul used to be. But then that father was desperate. So I can see why people who'd got nothing to lose would try Jesus. After all, if you're already an outcast, or if the person you love best is dying, then why not risk it?

'But Paul wasn't like that. He was really well educated, born and brought up a Jew, and put a lot of energy into becoming a real expert. He had a respectable trade, and a good reputation. He told me that when he first heard about the Christians, he hated them, because they seemed to be undermining all he'd worked for. He actually helped to persecute them, and when he first came to believe, they didn't trust him an inch, which is hardly surprising. Actually, I suspect that some of them are still not really sure about him.

'So what made him turn everything around, and give up his family and his comfortable life and start travelling all over the world, preaching about Jesus? More often than not, he got beaten up, or chucked out of the town, but he never gave up, and gradually the faith is spreading all over the world, thanks to him, and others like him.

'He spent quite a lot of time thinking about how his old religion and his new religion fitted together. I remember copying out passages about Abraham, and about how what's special about Abraham is that he trusted God, as though God was some kind of a friend he could rely on, rather than one of the old gods, whose whims you just had to put up with, or one who only cared if you'd done what you were told. Faith, that's what Paul kept going on about. Nobody can keep the law, he used to say, however hard they try, but anyone can get to know God and trust him, just like Abraham did.

'Of course, if all they say about Jesus is true, then there's good reason to trust, because Jesus's resurrection means life for all of us. But what if it's not true, I remember asking Paul once. I thought he would be angry with me, but he just smiled and said that he knew, better than anyone, how true it was, because he'd met the Risen Lord, and it had changed his life. He said that he hadn't realized how desperate he was. He thought his life was just fine, the way it used to be. But when he met Jesus, he knew that anything outside Jesus wasn't really life at all.'

Proper 6

—— ∾ ——

Exodus 19.2–8a
Romans 5.1–8
Matthew 9.35—10.8

Christians know that, through the work of God in Christ, made real
to them by the Holy Spirit, the world is a different place. We are, to
use Paul's characteristic phrase, 'justified by faith', through no merit
or action on our part. But what does that feel like, and what does
it mean?

In chapter 4, Paul has given a long and complex theological
explanation of 'justification by faith', and how this is not a new
departure in God's relations with us, but is characteristic of all
God's dealings with us. Now Paul turns from abstract to concrete.
So you are justified by faith. What does that feel like? According to
Paul, it feels like the end of a war. We are now at peace with God.
It is easy to think of peace as an inner state of quietude, but that
can't be what Paul is talking about, if you read the next few verses,
and if you know anything about his life. Peace, for Paul, is not a
feeling, but an actual change in the world. He has known what it is
like to be at war with God, fighting against what he knew, at some
level, was God's work in Jesus. He has known what it was to be in
an uneasy and mistrustful truce with God, when he tried to do
God's will, but failed, over and over again. Peace with God is
knowing that you are on the same side as God, for ever. God has
sent his ambassador, Jesus, to grant you citizenship. Whatever you
do or fail to do from now on, you have rights, a passport, that
signals that you are at peace with God's kingdom.

So the characteristic of a justified Christian, according to Paul, is
not a serene smile, but hope. Your passport is stamped 'nationality:
Christian', and you know that that is more or less the equivalent of
saying 'nationality: alive'. Everything that happens to you from
now on proves where you belong. Everything is characteristically
'Christian'. So it may be 'British' never to talk to people on trains,
and we have a kind of embarrassed pride in our reserve. Similarly,

it is characteristically 'Christian' to suffer. This is not something we worry about, but something we see as a 'national' characteristic. Hope is the beginning and end of our journey. We start out on it, our passport as justified citizens of God's kingdom clutched in our hands, because of what God has done for us and promised to us in Jesus. We trace with pride the way in which our national Spirit grows in us as we travel, our likeness to the archetypal 'Christian', Jesus himself, brought more and more to the fore by this Spirit of Christianity.

But this citizenship is not ours by right of birth or marriage or residence, but simply because the ruler of this nation goes out and searches for his people. We set out in hope, and the more we travel, the more we understand the nature of hope, God's great act of hope in Christ. God simply decides that we are his people. While we still think we are at war with God, he has already decided that we will carry his 'nationality'. But instead of conquering us to make us his own people, he allows us to conquer him. And when we find that we have no prison strong enough to hold him, whether that prison is made of hatred, or fear or death itself, God does not go free, mocking us for our efforts. Instead, he takes us with him into freedom.

But if we accept this passport, this citizenship into life, we must also accept the Spirit that goes with it. You cannot be citizens of God's kingdom without the Spirit of the kingdom, which is the Spirit of hope. God's hope is based on his unswerving love for us, which we can do nothing to alienate, which we do nothing to deserve. But once you accept that passport into freedom and life, you must accept that this Spirit of hope will increasingly form your being. This Spirit will begin to shape all your decisions, the way you respond to other people, the way you see life. You will not be able to do or be anything that does not proclaim your citizenship. Sometimes, admittedly, your fellow citizens may be ashamed of you, or see you as a failure, but that will not mean that you have forfeited the rights that the ruler gave you. You may even feel that you could share some of your rights, as the King did, by offering to end the wars you may be involved in. Not an uncostly business, but one full of God's hope.

Proper 7

— ∾ —

Jeremiah 20.7–13
Romans 6.1b–11
Matthew 10.24–39

The prophet Jeremiah lived through times of enormous political upheaval. His long career, lasting about 40 years, saw a good king, a couple of bad kings, a weak king and the forced deportation of all but the dregs of the population. Most of this Jeremiah warned his people about in advance, but his foresight won him no friends at all. He was increasingly isolated from the people he was born to serve, and at times his life was threatened by those who could not bear to hear that the truth was so different from what they wanted.

It was not as though Jeremiah had any choice about his calling. At the beginning of the book (1.5), we hear God telling Jeremiah that, even while he was a foetus, he was being prepared for the role of God's prophet. Perhaps he could have refused to pass on what God gave him to say – resisting a vocation is not unknown, after all – but in today's lament, Jeremiah cries out that not to speak is as painful as the fear and loneliness that follows after he has spoken. It burns him up, and the pain of holding it in becomes too much (v. 9). (Actually, it sounds a bit like childbirth – you don't want to push because it hurts too much, but the force is irresistible.) Nor does Jeremiah have any choice about what it is he has to say. God only gives him words of 'violence and destruction' (v. 8), however much he longs to speak love and reassurance.

So the words we hear from Jeremiah today are words of deep depression and despair. Jeremiah almost hates God, though he is at least honest about that. He accuses God of lying to him and forcing his words on him. The words are so strong that it is almost as though Jeremiah sees God's action as rape. All around him, he hears whispers, sees shadows, any one of which could mean his death, except that the God who assaults him is also the one who protects him from others.

And if verses 12 and 13 remind us that this horrible picture of

Jeremiah's relationship with God is only one side of the story, still it is a side we need to hear, while remembering that there is no hint of condemnation from God for what Jeremiah is feeling. Perhaps God recognizes something of the truth of the accusations Jeremiah is levelling against him. If Jeremiah's people had listened to the word of God, of course, Jeremiah's whole life could have been different. But at the moment it is not the stupid, self-serving people that Jeremiah hates, but the God who calls him to serve them, whether they will listen or not.

Christian disciples throughout the centuries have faced similar moments, as Jesus warned them they would. Like Jeremiah, they have to tell the people what they are given to tell, and most of the time their audience do not want to hear it, any more than the people of Judah did. Like Jeremiah, they cannot choose to soften the message if it is not to people's liking, not even if those people are their own families. Like Jeremiah, knowing that God protects them, and that they are 'of more value than many sparrows' (v. 31) to him, will not always be a great consolation. Sometimes, like him, they will long for ordinary friends, for family life, for simple pleasures, without the awful responsibility of being God's chosen ones. The life that God offers will seem very far away and unreal compared to the life they are obviously forfeiting.

That is why Paul is incredulous when he realizes that some people have heard his message of God's free grace as a signal that they can do what they like and get away with it. True, God's forgiveness is freely offered; it does not have to be earned, and it never can be. But accepting it means stepping out of one life into another, and there is only one way to do that. Stepping out of this life into the life of the crucified and risen Christ may seem like a good idea when you are wretched at your own sin and failure, but when you then have to follow in Christ's footsteps, you begin to wonder if you have made the right choice after all. 'Not peace, but a sword', 'our old self crucified', the Lord, a 'dread warrior', constantly beside you. Is this what you chose?

Hear God's silent acceptance of Jeremiah's scream of pain, see that the face of the 'dread warrior' is also the face of Jesus, and remember that the old life had moments like this too, but then they were meaningless. Now they are part of God's living purpose.

Proper 8

— ∾ —

Jeremiah 28.5–9
Romans 6.12–23
Matthew 10.40–42

Ours is an age with a great deal of interest in 'spirituality'. We have rediscovered that 'spirituality' is good for us and, like exercise and a low-fat diet, we pursue it, but on the whole rather sporadically. It becomes another way of paying attention to ourselves, and trying to meet our own needs, but we do not allow it to make demands upon us or inconvenience us too much.

There is really remarkably little in the way of this kind of spirituality in the Bible. It may have been what Hananiah was offering. I see him as a kind of Californian guru, or a tele-evangelist. He looks at all the anxious, stressed people, and he wants to help them. And if, by some lucky accident, that leads to wealth and favour for himself, well, whoever said that God wants us to be miserable? That poor man Jeremiah really should get himself some therapy, and not lay his guilt trips on other people.

Perhaps Hananiah really did believe that he was speaking God's word into the situation, but he seems much more interested in the personal psychology of his listeners, their needs and fears. Jeremiah, on the other hand, is operating out of a different theology of spirituality and prophecy. For Jeremiah, the only imperative is God's. He, personally, would much prefer to be carrying Hananiah's message of victory and peace but, unfortunately, it doesn't happen to be true. Jeremiah expects his prophecy to have cash value – it will be proved. Does Hananiah expect that too? Or is that secondary to him? Is he really just going for the feel-good factor, and not expecting to be held to account for it? It is as though that woolly layer of living, in which most talk of 'spirituality' exists, is ripped away by Jeremiah. 'This is not about what we want,' he shouts, 'this is about what actually is.'

The same kind of horrible immediacy confronts us in Jesus's words in Matthew. We cannot just pursue what is good for us on and off. On the days where we lapse from our diets, or don't go to the gym, or don't get the feng shui of our houses quite right, we can always start again tomorrow. But every day, in everything we do, we are right up against God. Scarlett O'Hara's attitude – 'tomorrow is another day' – probably won't even work with diets. It does suggest a fundamental lack of commitment, even there. But if you are talking about missing opportunities to meet and serve your maker and redeemer, it becomes a little more serious. Jesus is putting it positively in this passage, speaking of opportunities taken, rather than missed; but you can't help thinking of the other side.

Paul, too, has no time for spirituality as a lifestyle choice. Choice is certainly involved, but Paul is clear that your choices shape you so completely that slavery is the only appropriate description of the relationship between you and what you have chosen. Most of us in the privileged West, most of the time, treat our choices as ephemeral – after all, we can always choose again. But Paul is arguing strongly against that kind of free-market spirituality and theology. Every time you choose in favour of one thing, you choose against another. You cannot have it all. What you choose today becomes your master. It directs and controls you, as surely as if you were branded and wore an iron hoop around your ankle. What you choose today will make it harder to choose differently tomorrow.

Luckily, Paul's gospel is the good news of God's redeeming work in Christ, which does indeed allow us to choose again, and which frees us from the power of all our other choices. The good news is that God chooses us. Intriguingly, Paul still calls this 'slavery'. Jeremiah could testify that to choose God is no less demanding than choosing self. But perhaps, too, Paul is saying something vital about the strength and passion of our choosing of God. It must at least equal the strength and passion with which we choose what we eat, what we wear, what we worry about, otherwise it will never prevail. So deeply are we enslaved to 'sin' that only a really strong and opposing enslavement can make any difference. This is what John Donne is talking about when he beseeches God to 'Batter my heart . . . Take me to you, imprison me, for I/ unless you enthrall me, never shall be free,/ nor ever chaste except you ravish me.'[1]

If it makes us uncomfortable to think of being God's slaves, that is perhaps because we seldom admit how much we are enslaved to other things already. Even 'spirituality' can enslave. Only slavery to God is freedom.

---

[1] John Donne, 'Holy Sonnets', *The Oxford Book of English Verse*, OUP, 1972, p. 198.

Proper 9

—— ∼ ——

Zechariah 9.9–12
Romans 7.15–25a
Matthew 11.16–19, 25–30

The first half of chapter 11 of Matthew's Gospel is Jesus's tribute to John the Baptist. John is in prison, longing to know if he has stepped aside for nothing, aching to be reassured that he has truly listened to God. He gets the reassurance he needs and then Jesus turns to the crowd and says his public 'Thank yous' to John, the man who was prepared to be nothing so that Jesus could step into his rightful place.

But the crowd aren't really very interested. After all, John is yesterday's news. They have already moved on to the next sensation. The tabloids are full of Jesus, for the moment, until he puts a foot wrong, or something more interesting and less demanding turns up. They are getting restless with all this talk about John. They have come to hear about themselves, their needs, their hopes and fears. Who cares about that old has-been, John?

Jesus knows them well, as his ironic little parable shows. They are like selfish children, who will only play their own game, and even then, only if they can take the main part. When their fellow playmates, John and Jesus, try to initiate a game, the bored children won't play. 'I don't like that game,' they shout, 'I didn't make it up, and I don't like it. It's a silly game.' 'Your game is too sad,' they tell John, 'why can't we play a happy game? Someone's always dying in your game.' 'And your game is too noisy,' they tell Jesus, 'and I. don't like that kind of cake, and you've got more squash than I have.'

But of course, the end result for these poor, cross, dissatisfied children is that they have no one to play with at all, and no idea of how or what to play on their own. They are alone, crying and grumpy, not knowing what they really want, only that they haven't got it.

But if the spoiled, tantrum-throwing child is one half of today's picture the other half is the excited, curious, wondering child of verses 25–7. This is the child who does not always need to be in charge, but who is happy to play the game by someone else's rules. This is the child who has not been left alone with only other children to try and sort things out by themselves, but whose Father is there to play too. His Father will not force the game; he will allow the child to take it in his own direction, but he will be there, sharing, enjoying, rejoicing in the imagination and creativity of his child.

The intimacy of these verses is very moving, with their repeated use of the child's voice calling on the 'Father'. When we move into the final few verses of this chapter of Matthew 11, what we hear is this voice again, but now grown up. It is the voice of the child who has been well fathered, who has known the love and support and delight of his father, and can now in turn care for others. Jesus, the child of the Father, turns to those spoiled lonely children from the earlier verses, and offers them rest. The burden of their discontent and frustration is too much. Can they learn to turn to the Son of the Father?

Paul is certainly tired of trying to play on his own, and is more than ready to accept the rest offered by Jesus. Paul could sympathize with those children who reject all the games they are offered, but then have nothing left to do. He understands perfectly well that the children are rejecting happiness. If only they could forget themselves and play, they would be happy, but some inner stupidity and pride won't let them. They know quite well what they want – they want to play with the other children, but only on their own terms. They know that they have deliberately cut themselves off from what they want. Nobody else made them do it; they chose to sulk and shout. They chose to be miserable when they wanted to be happy.

Paul has longed for the parent who would come and tease and laugh and start a new game that could persuade all the children to forget their pride and their grudges and play together. And now he has found what he was looking for all his life – a way to forget himself and so be what he wants to be. Julian of Norwich writes of this experience in her *Revelations of Divine Love*. 'God, of your goodness, give me yourself ... If I ask for anything less, I shall always be in want. Only in you do I have all.'[1]

---

[1] Julian of Norwich, *Revelations of Divine Love*, Penguin, 1966, p. 68.

Proper 10

—— ∽ ——

Isaiah 55.10–13
Romans 8.1–11
Matthew 13.1–9, 18–23

Why is God so profligate? With the second half of today's reading from Matthew, the emphasis switches from God's action to our response; but the first half of the story is all that the listening crowds get, and their reaction must have been one of incredulity. Jesus's audience may not all be farmers themselves, but they would all be much closer to the food-production cycle than most of us are. They would have known famine and shortage, and they would know that a sensible farmer does not just fling the seeds all over the place. He prepares the ground as well as he can in advance, precisely so that the seeds don't fall on rocky ground or among thorns. Whatever is this sower in the story up to?

No wonder the disciples need an explanation. The one that they got has provided generations of Sunday-school lessons, with the emphasis on how we receive the word of God, so generously scattered abroad. But it is still an immensely puzzling story. For one thing, it is hard to see what those who hear God's word are supposed to do about it. It isn't clear that any blame attaches to them. For instance, can it be entirely their own fault if they don't understand what is being said to them? I suppose the shallow people, and the ones who allow themselves to be distracted by 'the cares of the world and the lure of wealth' could be said to deserve what they get, up to a point.

But I still think the sower is really the key. It is the sower who starts the story, and the explanation is given to those who are going to be 'sowers'. God may be the primary sower, but the disciples have accepted the commission to join Jesus in spreading the word far and wide, so it is their duty to make sure that the soil is prepared, that the birds are scared away, that the thorns are uprooted, and that the seed does not fall where there is not enough soil to let it grow. The disciples are being given the key, not to make them feel superior, and to assure them of their status in the inner circle, but so that they can be responsible for those who have no other means of hearing the Word. This is not, then, primarily a parable for seed, which is, by its very nature, bound to grow or fail, depending where it is put. No, this is a parable for the sowers.

But if this sounds like too terrifying a responsibility, then take Isaiah and Romans to heart. Although for some inexplicable reason God chooses to involve us in his mission, and to give us real responsibility, he knows what we are. God's word will 'accomplish that which I purpose', says God through Isaiah, 'and succeed in the thing for which I sent it'. How very hard it is always to believe that. We long to take over from God, to bend him to our purposes. We are sure that we know best. We would not be the sower who flings the seed about without looking where it is going to land. We would make sure that the seed got only to the people like us, that we know can be trusted with it. How different our careful, defensive, well managed strategies are from God's wild randomness.

So when Paul says that there is 'now no condemnation for those who are in Christ Jesus', those of us who are trying so hard need to hear it, as much as anyone else. After all, people who don't care about the law at all are not the ones who fear breaking it inadvertently. It is those of us who are zealously law-abiding who need freedom. Both sets need forgiveness, but Jesus's ministry showed, over and over again, that it is those who are trying to be righteous who find it hardest to accept that forgiveness.

But if, on one level, this is reassuring for anxious sowers, on another, it is even more terrifying than the responsibility of sowing God's word. Because Paul also says that 'the mind that is set on the flesh is hostile to God'. He does not say that such minds have to be doing or thinking evil, but simply that they are, in themselves, hostile to God. All God's values are anathema to them. They cannot stand the generous profligacy of the Spirit.

So what must we wishful sowers do? Prepare the ground as much as we can, but then trust in the generous mercy of God, and sometimes throw caution to the wind, and watch with delight as God's word accomplishes what we could never have dreamed of.

Proper 11

—— ❧ ——

Isaiah 44.6–8
Romans 8.12–25
Matthew 13.24–30, 36–43

This section of Romans is part of a long and not always lucid discussion of life and death, slavery and freedom. In chapter 6, Paul has been explaining that our Christian baptism means choosing Jesus's death and life rather than our own. On the whole, this choice is glorious for us. It means that we are no longer tied to sin and bound to do what sin tells us and pay the terrible price that follows. So it is freedom and life. But there are ongoing consequences from our previous life which sometimes make it hard for us to remember our new-found freedom. Sometimes we still act like slaves, rather than free people.

Then in chapter 7 Paul gives an illustration which is supposed to show what a good thing the death of the old life is. Once somebody is dead, the duties and debts you owed them are cancelled, Paul argues. So when you choose the death and life of Christ as your own, you are free of the things that bound you in your old life.

Finally, in chapter 8, Paul is looking at mechanisms – how does Jesus's death and life free us, and what does our freedom mean in practice? Paul's simple, compelling answer is that our freedom means life. When we 'belonged', body and soul, to the old life, that meant that we had to pay all the bills, fulfil all the demands of that life, and the final payment was our own death. But now we belong to God, body and soul, and God has a different way of demanding payment. Instead of asking us to pay, God gives us things. We thought we were being bought in the slave market by a new master, though admittedly one who would be nicer to us than the old. But instead we find that God has bought us so that he can make us his children, giving us equal shares in his property with his own Son. And what's more, the Son doesn't mind, and isn't jealous, but is actually the one who has gone out and done the buying, expressly so that he can share what should have been his.

Most of the time we can hardly believe it. We still keep looking over our shoulders, waiting for the beating. We still have the furtive, scared, selfish habits of the slave. But the third member of our new family is coaching us, gradually, teaching us the language of our new household, persuading us that it is really all right to speak to our owner as the Son does.

But if this is a wonderful new life for us – which it is – it does, unfortunately, carry some responsibilities with it. If we are going to talk like the Son, we also have to act like the Son. And until we do, the rest of the world cannot be free.

The problem is that when we set out to try to share our freedom with the world, we often revert to our old slave mentality. Isn't it interesting in the parable in Matthew that it is the slaves who want to uproot the weeds? The slaves have never owned anything themselves, but they are sure that if they did they could not stand to have it contaminated by weeds. The slaves would be prepared to put in any amount of back-breaking labour to uproot the weeds, even if it did mean damaging some of the crops at the same time. They are anxious, indignant, perhaps even a little fearful that the master will blame them for what has happened. In other words, they are acting like the slaves they are.

But the master's attitude is very different. The master's main concern is to preserve the crop. Separating out good and bad growth can more safely be done when the crop is fully grown. It's not that he doesn't mind about the weeds, or that he has any intention of pretending that they are anything else; it's just that he can take the long-term view, and the slaves can only worry. They are used to small, everyday tasks, with immediate results; they are not used to large, long-term responsibilities.

So what happens when the slaves suddenly become the children, and when the crop they are talking about is their own inheritance, and doesn't just belong to someone else? Will they panic and try to go for a completely weed-free field, whatever the cost? Or will they have lived with the master long enough to learn to think like him, and even to trust his strategies more than their own?

With creation still wrapped in the chains that we can still remember and feel around us, can we learn to act as children, not slaves?

Proper 12

—— ❧ ——

1 Kings 3.5–12
Romans 8.26–39
Matthew 13.31–33, 44–52

With this piling up of images of the kingdom, I think you need first of all to listen to them and get an overall feel, and then to start trying to tease out some of the puzzles. After all, those who heard the stories in the first place could not have sat down and read and reread them, but a good story makes you go on thinking for ages afterwards. Clearly, the crowds who followed Jesus everywhere he went did so at least partly for the stories. Who knows how they told and retold them, for years afterwards, as we still do?

So, first impressions? Unpredictability and excitement. Small things, that only one or two people know about, that suddenly swell and take over the world. Beautiful and incredibly valuable things that you come across by accident and can't live without.

The two sets of parables seem initially to lead in slightly different directions. The mustard seed and the yeast are everyday miracles. Everyone knows how they work, and how extraordinary it is that something so small can have such an effect. But had you ever thought of the kingdom of heaven like that? Surely the kingdom of heaven is already huge and magnificent, not something tiny, working inconspicuously until suddenly you can't miss it any more? The surprise in these parables is not what the yeast and the mustard seed do, since we know about that already. The point is that other things, that you may not be so familiar with, may also behave like this. Don't discount small things until you know what they are capable of. Don't think about big things as though they can never have had small beginnings.

The parables of the treasure and the pearl, on the other hand, feed straight into the imagination. Who hasn't dreamed of finding treasure? But the odd thing about both of these lucky people is what they do with it. Most people's treasure dreams are dreams about wealth, but these two have dreamt of the beauty of the treasure itself, and what it would feel like to know it was yours. Both of them seem to be reasonably well off already – they have things that they can sell in order to gain possession of the treasure, and there is absolutely no suggestion that they intend to sell what they have bought in order to get even richer. In fact, they might even appear to their neighbours to have lost their wealth. But little do the neighbours know.

(The parable about the fish seems to belong with the one about the crop sown with weeds, but it does serve to remind us, in this context, that treasure – or fish – are not always what they seem.)

What holds together the parables of sudden growth and the parables of treasure is the scribe in verse 52. He is the disciples and he is us. He is the one who has to use these stories to plant small ideas that will feed the world, he is the one who has to show that the treasure is so beautiful that it is worth selling all that we have to possess it. He has to ask people God's question to Solomon, 'What do you really want, more than anything else in the world?' Solomon's answer makes it clear that he already possesses, at least in part, what he has asked for.

Luckily, Paul tells us, so do we. Ours is not innate wisdom, but the presence of the Spirit, who can tell God what we meant to ask for, if only we had the sense to recognize our deepest longings. And what is this thing that we yearn for so deeply that we can hardly identify it, except to know that without it we are incomplete? It is, Paul tells us, to know that we are loved, completely, inalienably and for ever. God has had plans for us from the very beginning. He never intended his Son to be an only child. We are not an accident for whom sudden and unexpected alterations had to be made. God prepared his extensive nurseries from the beginning, and he knew that wipe-down surfaces would be necessary. We, with all that we entail, are God's choice. He knew what we would be like, and how expensive we would be, and he didn't care. God is prepared for everything that such parenthood involves.

So never listen to anyone who tells you that you are just adopted, and God wishes he hadn't done it. Don't believe a word if they try to say that God's love is conditional and might be forfeited. Don't see adversity as a sign that God has gone away. Simply stick with the Son, your brother.

Proper 13

—— ❦ ——

Isaiah 55.1–5
Romans 9.1–5
Matthew 14.13–21

The pain in Paul's words is tangible, and made even more poignant by the victorious assurance of the end of chapter 8. Paul has just been asserting that nothing can 'separate us from the love of God in Christ Jesus our Lord', and now, suddenly, we move into this howl of lament. For one moment he allows himself to dwell on something that seems to contradict what he has just said, because something has separated his fellow Israelites from the love of God, apparently. How can these things be reconciled? Has Paul got it wrong, after all? He can only search the depth of his knowledge of Christ, confirmed, he believes, by the Holy Spirit. And remember his description of the Holy Spirit in chapter 8, as the one whose voice is increasingly heard in us, drawing us into true conversation with God. So when he now speaks of an inner confirmation from the Holy Spirit, he is not speaking simplistically of a 'personal conviction', but of the discipline born of the years in which he has tried, increasingly, to hear the conversation between God and God, going on in him and around him, to hear it, submit to it, and play his own part in it. This 'confirmation' comes as a result of the whole of Paul's Christian life, given to God, without counting the personal cost.

And yet, and yet . . . Paul cannot simply turn away from the love of his people. For all the years of his childhood and early manhood, until he was confronted by Jesus on the road to Damascus, love of his people and fierce pride in their role in God's purposes are what shaped Paul's life. There is no easy road from one allegiance to another. It makes it almost harder that Paul still retains deep respect for his former people. It might be simpler if he could just say, 'They're wrong and I'm right.' But he can't. He acknowledges the value of all that has been given to the Israelites. They are real gifts, not an illusion, and they really play their part in God's purposes, all leading up to that great moment when the Messiah comes. And that is the rub, because those great gifts should have prepared the people to recognize Jesus, but somehow the people mistook the signs for the reality.

The problem, as Paul works it out in the rest of this tortured chapter, did not stop with the Israelites. It remains a common human desire to tie God down. We may even be trying to make the knots out of real rope, made by God and given to us by him. But we are doomed to failure if we are relying on anything other than God himself. You have to trust in God, his generosity and mercy, not any righteousness you think you might have performed. Even if that righteousness is called out of you in response to what God has done, still you must trust the God who called it from you, not your own acts.

And if you do, Matthew and Isaiah suggest, then suddenly God's wild generosity bursts the banks of the little channel in which you thought you were sailing, and you are out on the huge, uncharted, enchanting seas of God's love for the world he has made. When the disciples come to Jesus and ask him to send the people away, they think that they are being thoughtful and kind. Jesus came out to be on his own, and he has been mobbed, so – first kind thought – let's carve out a bit of space for Jesus. Second kind thought: the people have come a long way, and they are going to start getting tired and hungry any minute now. For their sakes, too, it's time they went home. Notice the disciples carefully not mentioning their own needs.

At first it looks as though, in response to their kindness, Jesus is giving them an impossible task. 'You feed them,' he says. But actually, all he is asking is one small response – just five loaves and two fishes – and Jesus is the one who will make it bread for five thousand. 'You feed them' is only daunting if you don't trust in the generosity of God. 'Come and buy,' Isaiah shouts. You could look longingly at the things set out on God's stall and decide you can't afford them, count your few pennies and go and buy something inferior, or you could approach God, hold out your empty purse, your empty hands, and have them filled to overflowing. The stewards of God's stall must not spend their time bargaining, but instead give the goods away as fast as we can, knowing that they will always be replenished.

Proper 14

—— ~ ——

1 Kings 19.9–18
Romans 10.5–15
Matthew 14.22–33

There is something about us that is deeply resistant to the grace of God. It's not that we don't believe in him, or wish to follow him, or that we consciously reject him, but we simply cannot help reverting to the belief that all of this is something 'we' do, something we have to achieve with our own efforts. We act as though God is far away and a hard taskmaster, who has to be won over by our grim attempts to read his mind and so please him.

For once, in Romans 5, Paul is making a direct comparison between the law and justification by faith. Usually he is at pains to say that the law is not innately bad, it's just that we are not capable of keeping it. But here he is comparing what he sees as the attitude behind these two ways of approaching God. The law, he says, is about doing things. It is about a kind of credit and debit account that God keeps, so that you might, theoretically, end up in credit, but the chances are strongly against it.

Faith, on the other hand, is an acceptance of what God has done, in sending Jesus and raising him from the dead. All of that was done without any effort or even consent on our part, and all we have to do in response is recognize it as the activity of God. So Paul counsels against turning faith into a new kind of strenuous pursuit, where you have to search out God and grab him to you by force. God is closer to you than your own breath and heartbeat.

But Peter shows how very hard it is to believe that. Chapter 14 marks a change of pace in Matthew's Gospel. Jesus's ministry is about to come into the full public gaze, as it begins to really worry both Herod and the Pharisees. Jesus is trying to carve out a little space for himself, to pray and reflect and gird himself up for the confrontations to come. Finally, after the feeding of the five thousand, he persuades the disciples to go off in the boat and leave him alone. I wonder what the conversation was like in the boat that night? They must all have been very excited by the miracle they had just been part of, and full of enthusiasm and hope. But as the storm begins to get up, and they are still hanging around waiting for Jesus, they begin to lose heart.

Typically, it is Peter whose enthusiasm returns immediately. As soon as he sees Jesus, he wants another dose of the high excitement of miracles, and Jesus indulges him. But out on the unstable water, with the wind even stronger without the protection of the boat around him, Peter panics. He had thought miracles were a kind of magic, that would make the waves feel like a road, and build a shield around him to keep the wind off. He had thought of Jesus's power as some kind of almost external force, to be tapped and used as he pleased. He had not realized that Jesus's power is not magic, but the absolute demonstration of nature responding to her maker. Peter had set out to do exactly what Paul was talking about – to try to get close to God's power by sheer force of will. Instead, he has to reach out his hand to Jesus, and recognize that he walks on the water as a disciple of Jesus, not by any other kind of power at all.

So the disciples' response is, at last, the right one. 'You are the Son of God,' they say to Jesus, as their boat rocks calmly on the friendly sea.

Christianity is not a system, which some people can use easily and some can't, and each person can only reap the rewards accordingly. Christianity is a relationship, offered by God, in which our place is opened up by Jesus, and in which we are constantly tutored and encouraged by the Holy Spirit. No one is 'good' at it, but that's all right, because entrance is not by exam, and places are not limited. The temptation is to go off looking for challenges to prove your worth to God, or seeking him in the terrifying power of the wind, the earthquake and the fire, because surely silence and the rhythm of your own heart are too small and mundane for God? Elijah, the disciples and Paul have all seen the spectacular power of God, but they all learn to be much more awed by God's offer of intimacy than by any other kind of demonstration. In the end, what more could we want?

Proper 15

———— ∼ ————

Isaiah 56.1, 6–8
Romans 11.1–2a, 29–32
Matthew 15.10–28

This strange story of the Canaanite woman clearly scratches an itch for Matthew's readers. If you put this version and Mark's version side by side (Mark 7.24–30), you will see some subtle differences. Mark's version is, as usual, more abrupt, but both can be read on at least two levels.

The first level is the main strand of the story. Both Gospels put this interchange between Jesus and the foreign woman in the context of an increasingly angry and critical set of encounters with the Pharisees and scribes. The Pharisees are questioning Jesus's authority, and he in turn is challenging their understanding of the Law, and so of God. But although Jesus argues forcefully and with confidence, he is essentially arguing in terms that the Pharisees understand. This whole debate is conducted in the language of scriptural interpretation, with each side determined to make its case. Jesus is clear that his mission is continuous with God's great missionary enterprise in calling the people of Israel, and the Pharisees are determined to show him that he is mistaken. But this is still very much a family fight, however bitter and potentially bloody. Who has the right to interpret the Tradition?

But then the Canaanite woman comes and begins to skew this plane of the story. However much Jesus has criticized the way in which his people have tried to tie God down, he has still seen his calling as within the family. But the woman won't let him. She challenges Jesus to see the full implications of what he has been saying to his own people.

In Mark, Jesus seems less thrown by her challenge. It is as though he had already realized that his mission had universal application, but had thought that there was an order to be observed – children first, then dogs. But here in Matthew, Jesus at first cannot formulate an answer for the woman at all. But neither can he turn her away, because surely she is right: she is not asking for the children's bread, only the leftover crumbs. And we readers, who have just come from the feeding of the five thousand in the previous chapter, and are about to go on to another miraculous feeding, smile at her cleverness. After all, we have just seen how many crumbs are left over when God has finished feeding the children – twelve baskets, wasn't it?

So this first level of the story is about Jesus coming to a fuller realization of the scope of his mission, and how typical of him it is that he instantly praises the woman for her insight. 'Great is your faith!' he says to her.

But the second level of the story is the one that operates for the reader, and this is where today's Gospel really connects with Paul's painful struggle in Romans. The earliest Christians, too, had to find out the breadth of their calling. Clearly, in the church for which Matthew was written there are those who believe that Christianity is primarily for God's original people, not for everyone. This is a battle that Paul had to fight over and over again, in his certainty that he was called to be 'an apostle to the Gentiles'.

In the end, Paul's theological resolution of this problem – never a complete resolution, but one that he can live with – rests on the faithful love of God. God does not call people in order to dismiss them later, and he does not give gifts and then ask for them back. But when his people do not respond to the call or want the gift, that does not render them useless. Instead, God uses that refusal as an opportunity, not to take the gifts away from their original recipients, but to give them more widely, in the hope that when the first recipients see others enjoying God's presents, they will blow the dust off their own and start joining in.

Now, of course, the proper context of this is the relationship between Christians and Jews, and it is vital for each side to hear that God intends to include us all in his great plan for our salvation. But if Christians think that is the end of it, then perhaps we need a Canaanite woman to come and ask us impertinent questions. Because the simple truth of the matter is that Christians, too, often fail to see the scope of what God has intended and will bring to pass. God's call is what brings us into being, and his gift is to make that being real, by sharing with us his own life. Whenever we are tempted to make Christianity something small and anxious, we need reminding that even God's crumbs can satisfy us completely.

Proper 16

———— ❧ ————

Isaiah 51.1–6
Romans 12.1–8
Matthew 16.13–20

There seems to be a bit of a break in the argument at this point in Romans. Chapters 9—11 are Paul's attempt to give some kind of coherent shape to God's activity in choosing first Israel and then all who believe through Christ. Now Paul is back to practical-sounding advice to the Christian community in Rome. Given the way in which ancient letters were written (dictated to a secretary) and preserved – read aloud and continually copied and recopied for wider distribution – it is hardly surprising that they don't always flow naturally from one paragraph to the next.

But actually the break is not complete. There is a logical progression from what Paul has been discussing in the last few chapters to this presentation of Christian ethics. The problem Paul identified with the law is that people put their trust in that rather than in God, and they believe that they can stand or fall by their own efforts. That attitude is not associated solely with the old covenant. On the contrary, it is the fall-back position of all humans in relation to God. 'Don't do it like that!' Paul begs his readers. 'Give yourself up, give yourself away, know that God is the active principle in all life, and dispense with the illusion that you are at the heart of everything.'

The great twentieth-century Protestant theologian, Karl Barth, calls Christian ethics 'the great disturbance'. In his commentary on Romans, Barth says that all human systems must inevitably be 'disturbed' by the thought of God.[1] God is not part of any of our systems, and none of them is capable of comprehending him. It is simply silly to think that we have the means of measuring and systematizing the creator of all that is.

Paul cuts straight through all the usual attempts to make moral systems that will allow us to continue our lives unchanged. Give your-

---

[1] Karl Barth, *The Epistle to the Romans*, OUP, 1968, p. 424.

Ordinary Time

self to God, Paul says, and that 'self' is not some abstract, theoretical inner being, but your real, physical self. 'Present your bodies' is one of Paul's annoyingly inescapable orders. Discipleship is like belonging to the army. You can't have long involved discussions about whether there is a proper time for Christians to wake up. Instead, you get up when the order is given, and you march where you are told. Not a theory, then, but a practice – the practice of discipleship.

If abstraction is one of the main temptations of ethics, the other is to love systems that correct other people's failings and leave your own untouched. And again, Paul is having none of it. Look squarely at your own strengths and weaknesses, and thank God that they are balanced out in the Christian community. Thank God that we are called together, and can help each other out, rather than having to have all the virtues in our own individual person.

Peter and the other disciples have been subjected to 'the great disturbance' since they first met Jesus. They are constantly having to revise their opinions of themselves, others and God in the light of Jesus's unsettling presence. Now, suddenly, Jesus puts them to the test. He starts with the easy question, the question about other people's opinions. All the disciples are happy to chip in, expounding all the theories they have heard about Jesus. But then comes the crunch question. 'Who do *you* say that I am?'

It isn't really a fair question. After all, the disciples are demonstrating, by their very presence, by all that they have given up, what they believe about Jesus. Why is he pressing them now to formulate it? His response to Peter gives the answer. To know who Jesus is is vital. It is not enough to believe that he is very important. It is not enough to believe that he is like the other prophets and messengers of God. When Peter declares 'You are the Messiah', he is saying what has to be said. Jesus is the key to the whole of God's relationship with what he has made.

On the basis of his confession – and on no other 'ethical' basis at all – Peter is made the rock on whom the Church is built. This, then, is to be our defining characteristic, our knowledge of Jesus Christ, and with that knowledge, we can open the gates of Heaven, and be unafraid of Hades.

Does it seem an adequate foundation for the Church? Shouldn't there be more rules and ethical norms laid down? How odd that Peter's sole qualification for the job – apart from a big mouth – is that he can recognize the activity of God when he sees it. Funnily enough, that's what Paul is working for too. 'Be transformed', he says, 'so that you may discern what is the will of God.'

Proper 17

———— ∿ ————

Jeremiah 15.15–21
Romans 12.9–21
Matthew 16.21–8

Oh dear. Now it's crunch time. Justification by grace through faith
is fine. A theology of grace alone, which emphasizes our inability to
achieve our own salvation, is central to Paul's faith, particularly as
expressed in this letter to the Romans. But it cannot be taken as
blanket permission never to change or strive. In today's passage,
Paul moves on from what we are not capable of to what he seems
to think we should be able to manage, and it is quite frightening.

The virtues Paul is asking the Christian community to exercise
are not the dramatic, noticeable ones, like heroism or courage in
battle, but the long-haul ones, for which we often get no praise, and
which have to be practised every minute of every day – love,
respect, patience, perseverance. But Paul knows that these are, in
fact, often the hardest and most trying skills to acquire. You do get
the impression, reading through his letters, that they didn't come
naturally to him, either. So it is surely no accident that he uses
emphatic and exaggerated language about these virtues. We are to
love with a passion, and hate the opposite of love, with equal
passion. We are to be competitively respectful, zealous in service,
joyful in hope, and almost embarrassingly hospitable. Paul needs
the Christian community really to understand that these qualities
will not come by accident. They have to be worked at with all the
dedication and energy that you would once have given to getting on
in the world, or being the best at your chosen sport.

He also needs them to understand that they cannot expect to be
loved and admired for their goodness. On the contrary, the better
they are at exercising these Christian virtues, the more they will
differ from the society around them, and the more they will be
disliked and persecuted. They must not expect understanding. No
one else will want to listen to their explanations of why they behave
as they do, and no one else will know that they are in the right. And

they simply have to put up with that. They must absolutely resist the temptation to take out full-page ads or hours of air time, telling the world 'we are right, and you are wrong'. No thought of getting their own back should ever enter their heads. This seems almost harder than anything else, to allow people to despise and dishonour us because we will not use their own weapons against them.

But we have it on very good authority that that is God's way. When the Son becomes incarnate, even the people he chooses as his closest friends do not understand him. Just before this passage from Matthew, Peter has made his enormous confession to Jesus – 'You are the Messiah,' he says, and Jesus blesses him. But his success seems rather to have gone to Peter's head. He seems to feel that he now has some kind of proprietary rights in Jesus's Messiahship, because here he is, telling Jesus off. 'No, no, you've got it wrong,' he says, 'a messiah doesn't lose. A messiah wins, and everybody worships him.' The savagery of Jesus's response just shows how very tempting it must have been. We assume that it was natural to Jesus to choose God's way, but the Gospels are full of suggestions that part of Jesus's identification with us is that, like us, he has to make his choice for God over and over again, every day. Of course he would have preferred to be Peter's kind of messiah. But unfortunately, that would simply have led to the perpetuation of violence and death. God's way is to bring life, but it can only be done by Jesus's completely unprecedented use of his power. He uses his power to love and to endure. So we know who our pattern is, when we come on to read Romans.

Listen to Jesus struggling to explain to his disciples why they must choose to follow his path. This is the way to life, the only way to life. Really, we do know this. We have only to look around at the history of a world governed by a different definition of power, and we see that the rulers are replaced by other rulers, that the governors die, just like the governed. No one can get their own way by force all the time. God's life is the only real and lasting life that there is, and he wishes to share it with us. At this point in Matthew, Peter has not got the point, but we know that he did, and that thanks to him and succeeding generations of Christians, we have a community that will help us to imitate Jesus.

Proper 18

—— ❧ ——

Ezekiel 33.7–11
Romans 13.8–14
Matthew 18.15–20

I suppose we can take comfort from the fact that today's passage from Matthew needed to be written at all, because you don't need to give advice where it is already being followed; but there the comfort ends. Clearly, there has never been a perfect, harmonious Christian community that needed no guidelines about how to handle disputes but, equally clearly, having guidelines doesn't make you observe them.

What is laid out here is the proper procedure when individual Christians fall out with one another. It starts with the private word, moves on to a small meeting and ends up with one person being estranged from the community. It is told from the point of view of the person who is in the right, but at every stage of the matter, there is the other story to be told. For example, suppose you are not the offended person, but the offending one. When your fellow Christian comes to complain about your behaviour, how do you react? Perhaps you genuinely do not see their point of view, and are convinced of your own innocence. But when they come back with a couple of others, who also agree that you are in the wrong, what then? Do you pause, think again, and try to change, or do you shout that of course their friends would agree with them, and go off and find some of your friends, who will be on your side? That will, of course, escalate things, and lead to divisions and cliques in the church.

What about at stage two of the procedure? Suppose you are convinced that someone has done something wrong, but after a private word with them, they won't admit it. You go off and return with some other Christians who are not directly involved in the dispute. You expect, of course, that they will be on your side. But what if they are not, or not as whole-heartedly as you would like? What if they see how the other person might not have meant what you think they did? What if they suggest a compromise? Do you insist on total surrender, at the risk of splitting the church, or will you agree, even if you are not convinced?

And then, of course, there is the final stage, where you have been proved right at every turn, and it is now clear that your fellow Christian is wrong, and not willing to change. You are now allowed to treat them like 'a Gentile and a tax-gatherer'. But what kind of treatment is that? Those words cannot be accidental, in a Gospel that has detailed Jesus's constant care for just those groups of people. This ex-Christian, who has put herself outside the Christian community, must now be treated to all your evangelistic powers to bring them back in. You have to show them the love and the care that Jesus showed to 'Gentiles and tax-gatherers'. You don't have time to feel smug about being right, you have work to do.

We cannot always be united, though we could probably manage it more often than we do. We must sometimes hold out for what we think is truth against falsehood, though probably less often than we would like. But against that temptation and need to squabble, we have the vision of what our unity might do. 'If two of you agree on earth about anything you ask, it will be done for you by my Father in heaven,' we are told, 'and, incidentally,' Jesus adds, 'I'll be there too.' There is a terrible sarcasm in that phrase 'if even just two of you could agree about anything'. What we forfeit by our love of discord!

Romans broadens this practical advice to include our general conduct, both to other Christians and to the world in which we live. Paul sounds almost impatient. Surely, he implies, any fool knows what we ought to be doing. Any law promulgated by any government can be summed up by the phrase 'love your neighbour'. Unfortunately, most of us are so clueless about what that might involve, or so determined to concentrate on only loving ourselves, that we need that spelt out a bit more. Pick yourself a concrete example, and work it through. It will actually involve some work, I'm afraid, and you may not see any results for a long time. I'm afraid loving your neighbour might involve you in finding out something about them. Would you like to be 'loved' abstractly, as though you had no personal qualities of your own? I thought not.

For Paul, this is not something to get round to one day, but a matter of extreme urgency. Rather a lot depends upon it. Ezekiel seems to agree.

Proper 19

— ∾ —

Genesis 50.15–21
Romans 14.1–12
Matthew 18.21–35

It is very annoying to think that God may have different standards of judgement from ours. All three of today's readings warn that the obvious surface reaction to one particular incident may turn out to be quite wrong, if you put it in the bigger context of what God is doing with the world.

Take the story of Joseph and his brothers, for example. There is no denying that his brothers treated him abominably, and even they do not try to excuse their behaviour. Even they realize that their reaction to an aggravating, spoiled little brother was completely out of proportion, and so they cannot quite believe in Joseph's forgiveness. Although they have been living safely and comfortably in Egypt for some time, under Joseph's influential protection, they still expect it to be withdrawn as soon as their father dies. They know what they have deserved from Joseph. But Joseph has seen the bigger picture. He has seen what God has done through the violent jealousy of the brothers, and he has seen that he was not the only one to benefit – all the Egyptian people who might have starved without Joseph's foresight can, in a strange way, plead for forgiveness for the people who unwittingly brought Joseph to Egypt.

In the parable that Jesus tells of the forgiven slave, again, you can see that the slave's mind was travelling in one direction, and he was forced to rethink. The slave sees the removal of the burden of debt as a chance to get his life straightened out. He will set all his financial affairs in order, and make sure that he never gets himself into that kind of debt again. Surely his master will approve of that? But his master's context was a bigger one. He was not thinking just about one slave and his money worries, but about the whole society of people he rules, whom he wishes to govern by example. He wanted the slave to see forgiveness in action and learn how to do it, so that more than one life could be put straight.

So both Joseph and the forgiven slave find out that what they initially thought was just about God and themselves turns out to have knock-on effects for many, many others. And that is what Paul is trying to say to the Romans. Of course there is an individual element to Christian obedience, but the point of it is not just to get our own life straight, but to demonstrate the power of the life of God in our midst.

Paul is writing this passage very carefully. Notice that he does not say that the 'weak' should wise up and start supplementing their vegetarian diet. Nor does he come down on one side or the other over days of observance. Each person must follow the path that God has given them, and they may actually be different yet equally obedient. It would be easy to read this passage as an endorsement of individualism and lazy liberalism. It really doesn't matter what you do, so long as you think it's all right. Love is all you need. But that isn't quite what Paul is saying. He is trying to get them to see the bigger context. This is not just about you and God, but about the sweep of God's saving activity in Christ. While you sit there, trying to force your own practices on other Christians, God is saving the world. Your small life will have ripples of consequences in God's great design. Will they be ripples flowing out from the huge impact of God's forgiving love in Christ, or just a very small eddy from a tiny, self-obsessed pebble, which has nothing to do with the tidal wave of God's love? Getting the big picture, that God in Christ wills to be 'Lord of both the dead and the living', does not necessarily make it easier to decide, day to day, how to live in obedience, but it does at least remind you why it matters.

At this time of year, inevitably, we are thinking about what happened in New York on September 11, 2001, and Paul's talk about forgiving a brother who won't eat meat seems irrelevant. But if we put these three passages together, in the bigger context they shout for, perhaps we in the West can see our society as one that is going to require a lot of forgiveness, and that might make us more careful in holding other cultures to account. What kind of reactions on our part might bring life out of death, might make an act of abominable violence a goad to the creation of a different society? How might we witness to our belief in the risen Lord of all?

Proper 20

—— ∾ ——

Jonah 3.10—4.11
Philippians 1.21–30
Matthew 20.1–16

Did Jonah ever get the point? The author deliberately chooses an open ending. Jonah knows his God quite well, but that doesn't mean he has to like him. He thinks God is ridiculously soft, but if God wants to make a fool of himself, that doesn't mean Jonah has to join in. As Jonah shouts at God, we finally find out why he ran away from God's commission in the first place: 'I know you, God,' Jonah shouts, 'I'll be preaching judgement, like you told me to, and then you'll go and forgive the people, and make me a look a fool.' And that is precisely what happens. In seconds, Jonah forgets how much he had relied on God's loving forgiveness to get him out of the belly of the whale or, if he doesn't forget, he doesn't see why these characteristics should not be reserved only for Jonah. Why does God have to be loving and forgiving to everyone?

Why does Jonah so hate the idea of God's forgiveness for others? It surely can't really be just about his own loss of face. After all, he has converted a whole great, sophisticated city to the way of the Lord. He must realize how he will be honoured and praised for it? So, no, this isn't really about Jonah's need to look big, but about his perception of justice. God should do what is just, and punish the wicked, otherwise who will ever take him – or his prophets – seriously again?

The people working in the vineyard, too, are a bit concerned about slipping standards. What this landowner is doing could create ill-feeling and unrest throughout the market place, with no one knowing what to expect. The people who had been working all day forget how glad they had been to see reinforcements, and how they had had to work less hard because of the extra help, and how the later workers had shared their food and drink, not having needed it themselves while they were standing around in the market place, waiting to be hired. They also forgot that they were still taking home a good day's wages to their families, and that the other workers had families too. Although they had got exactly what they bargained for, somehow it felt diminished because others also had it.

Like Jonah, the all-day workers forget that they needed first what God was now offering to others. In their case, they argue, it was their entitlement. But these others have not earned it, and should not have it. Jonah can't see a saved city, rejoicing in God and blessing the name of his prophet, because all he can concentrate on is what he thought God should have done instead. The all-day workers can't see the good day's wages, the well-picked vineyard, and the joy of the other workers at being able to feed their families, because they are too wrapped up with their own sense of grievance. Jonah could have dined out for months to come, fêted by the city he had saved, and the workers could all have gone to the pub together, and spent a little of what they'd earned, sharing a convivial evening, and telling stories about strange masters they'd worked for. But instead, they choose to be isolated and embittered. Philippians offers the alternative story, where people accept with gratitude what they are offered, and 'strive side by side'. Paul is not threatened because the Philippians are Christians too. On the contrary, he is thrilled. The Philippians are not angry about Paul's share of the limelight, but see him as an example, rather than a rival.

It is easy to see Jonah and the all-day workers as rather comic caricatures, responding as surely we never would to God's generosity to others. Which is why you have to take seriously not just their selfishness but also their concern about justice. Is Jonah not right to think that God will cheapen forgiveness, and will end up encouraging wrong-doing, because people can point out that God doesn't really seem to mind it much? Are the workers not right to suspect that the vineyard owner will have increasing trouble getting people to work for him all day, if they know they can turn up at the last moment and get a day's pay? In his brave and challenging book, *The Dignity of Difference*,[1] the Chief Rabbi, Jonathan Sacks, speaks, among other things, about what might happen if you dare to let go of the language of justice and rights, and speak instead in the language of 'covenant' and forgiveness. If God can bear to filter his justice through the lens of mercy, who are we to forget how much we have been forgiven, and demand harsh 'justice' for others?

---

[1] Jonathan Sacks, *The Dignity of Difference*, Continuum, 2002, pp. 202ff.

Proper 21

—— ∿ ——

Ezekiel 18.1–4, 25–32
Philippians 2.1–13
Matthew 21.23–32

'Don't forget the bring-and-buy sale next week; the ladies' group will meet on Thursday to continue their excellent work on the worn-out hassocks; and by the way, don't forget that Jesus Christ is the Son of God and saviour of the world.'

That's not really a fair parody of what is happening in Philippians, because the verses before the glorious hymn on the nature of Christ are not as mundane as a list of church notices, but even so, the effect is extraordinary.

Paul's relationship with the church in Philippi is beset with drama and danger. Acts tells us about the founding of the church, and how it led to beatings and imprisonment for Paul and Silas (you might like to refresh your memory by reading Acts 16.11–40). By the time he is writing this letter, Paul is back in prison. It isn't completely clear which of his many spells in prison this is, but it must have been quite lengthy, because there has been time for an exchange of letters, for people to visit, and for the Philippians to send Paul things to make him more comfortable and to further his work (see 4.10ff.).

Typically, Paul has used his imprisonment as a missionary opportunity. He tells us in 1.12ff. that his imprisonment is widely talked about and that it has made other Christians bolder in their own witness. This is part of what is feeding the great theme in chapter 2. Paul has had time to reflect on the fact that his enforced absence is actually releasing gifts in others. Perhaps his followers had come to rely too heavily on him to do the primary outreach, and they are now having to shoulder some of that responsibility themselves. When Paul talks about Jesus's humility and obedience 'to the point of death', he is acknowledging that his own powerlessness may also be serving God's purposes.

It is a hard truth for any leader to have to face, that your absence may be the best gift you can give your followers. But if there is a degree of anxiety in today's exhortation to unity, there is also considerable confidence. Paul is sure that he founded the church in Philippi on Christ, not on himself, and so he reminds them that there is really no problem about transferring their obedience. 'You've always obeyed me,' he reminds them in verse 12, 'but that obedience was really always obedience to God. Now you will have to cut out the middle man, and acknowledge that it was God who made you a Christian, not me.'

But while Paul wants the Philippian Christians to take a responsibility for their own lives and witness, he wants to make sure that this does not lead to fragmentation in the community. If they can't rely on Paul's authority to keep them together, will they start to fall apart? Or will they remember to model themselves on Christ, and be willing to submit themselves to God and each other?

Verses 6–11 are almost certainly not composed by Paul, but are part of a hymn to Christ that may have been quite well known in early Christian circles. The theology of the song is profound. It suggests that the 'proof' of Jesus's divinity is that he is prepared to give it up, in order to share our life and death. What marks Jesus as God is not anything we would normally recognize as 'power', except when we begin to recognize that it is a 'power' completely outside our own experience and abilities – the power to be utterly given to God.

It is one of the striking things about the Gospel accounts of Jesus, that he seems to be completely uninterested in power. Instead of building himself an army of followers, he sends most of them away. Instead of laying out his manifesto and insisting that God is on his side, he so often just refuses to answer any questions about himself. In today's Gospel, he easily resists the temptation to talk about himself and his authority, and instead begins to probe his questioners. What was their real reason for asking? What would constitute an 'authority' that they would recognize? The ironic little story of the two brothers is Jesus's answer to them. They need to learn to be obedient to God, nothing else.

In the context of the letter to the Philippians, the hymn to Christ might seem to use a sledgehammer to crack a nut. But Paul knows that you can never underestimate the human will to power. This fundamental insight about the nature of Christ is alien to us all. We need to learn to recognize the authority of God, and we have absolutely no other pattern for it, except Jesus.

Proper 22

— ∾ —

Isaiah 5.1–7
Philippians 3.4b–14
Matthew 21.33–46

The people listening to the story of the vineyard would have responded to it on a number of different levels. Some of them would have recognized this vineyard from Isaiah 5 and begun to make the connections from the beginning. The context in which Matthew puts this interchange assumes that the chief priests and Pharisees are a large part of the audience, and they would certainly be expected to hear the literary echoes. So they know, as soon as the story starts, that this is about God and Israel. But they are listening for the refinements, for the differences from the original, to see in which direction Jesus is taking the story. And they quickly spot the major difference, which is that this is not about what the vineyard has done wrong, as it is in Isaiah, but about the tenants. So, they guess, this is not going to be a story about judgement on the whole of Israel, but only some categories of people within it.

Others in the audience are listening to it with less educational baggage. They just want to find out what's happening in the actual story. To begin with, their sympathy is engaged with the landowner. They can imagine the hard, hot, back-breaking work that goes into clearing a piece of land and planting the vines. They can identify with the pleasure of the completed task. But then the landowner walks off, and the audience's sympathy begins to shift. All that work, and it turns out just to be a financial investment, they mutter. I wouldn't mind having so many vineyards that I could afford to let them out, they joke. Jesus's audience may not have been uniformly poverty-stricken, but the majority of them were probably more likely to have suffered from unpleasant landlords than unreliable tenants.

But these tenants are more than just a bit untrustworthy. They are mad. They are reacting with a violent and insane lack of logic, which culminates in their murder of the heir. Killing the slaves buys them a bit more time to enjoy the produce of the vineyard, so their mad calculations might just have led them to believe that there was some point to it. But their actions are completely oriented to the short-term. They don't stop to think about the increasingly heavy penalty they are earning for themselves. But their final act shows that long-term thinking is not within their capabilities at all. How can they ever have convinced themselves that killing the heir would make the vineyard theirs? Why is the owner suddenly going to make his son's murderers his heirs?

No, Jesus doesn't have to deliver the punchline to the story – all his audience know what is bound to happen.

But the reaction of the chief priests and Pharisees is extraordinary. Admittedly, their biblical knowledge would have helped them to the conclusion that they reach so quickly – that this is now a story about the leaders of the people – but, even so, you would expect them to reject Jesus's interpretation. 'We are not like that,' you would expect them to argue, 'that is a completely unfair characterization of us. We have always tried to give God his harvest. All our laws are set up to do just that. You're the one who is trying to keep the produce for yourself, not us.'

Would we so easily recognize ourselves as the villains of the piece? Admittedly this is not the vineyard story that Jesus would tell for us, exactly. The version of the story that we would hear might go like this. When the landlord sent to collect his produce, the tenants said, 'Of course, now, let's see, what is the correct procedure for this?' Or, 'We cannot agree about the best method for harvesting the grapes, and we cannot possibly work together until that is decided.' Or perhaps, 'Yes, indeed, but I'm afraid we had to sell all the grapes for the next twenty years in order to pay for the maintenance of the watch tower. As soon as that's under control, you shall have your produce.' Or, 'We're terribly sorry, but we couldn't get anyone to help us harvest the grapes, so they've all rotted on the vines. Could you just send us a few more helpers?'

Of course that is an unfair caricature, just as Jesus's story for the Pharisees was exaggerated and unfair. But Paul, at least, recognized enough truth in some such description of himself, and repented. All the credentials that he would once have trotted out as proof that he was the perfect tenant for God's vineyard he now realizes are worthless. There is only one thing he wants now, and that is to be more and more like Christ.

Proper 23

— ∽ —

Isaiah 25.1–9
Philippians 4.1–9
Matthew 22.1–14

This is an enigmatic little parable in Matthew. If you look at Luke's version of the story (Luke 14.15–24), you will see a much more straightforward narrative about the failure of those originally invited to realize the value of the invitation. The most striking difference between Matthew and Luke is the tone. Matthew's version of the story is full of urgency and bitter anger. It is only in Matthew that the banquet is completely ready and about to go to waste, and it is only in Matthew that the messengers are mistreated and vengeance exacted. And who is the mysterious guest without a wedding garment? He doesn't appear in Luke, but he adds an element of fear, so that there is no assurance of a happy ending, even for those who have made it to the banquet.

Part of the anger in the story is generated by the scene-setting opening verses. The King is throwing this party for his Son. The wedding banquet of the King's Son is a glorious and spectacular occasion for rejoicing, and most people would beg, borrow and steal to get themselves invited. But these strange people either don't care about the invitation at all, or else they treat it as a positive nuisance, to the point where they beat up the postman who brings the card. What should have been an occasion for national rejoicing is turned abruptly into a war zone.

There is bewilderment here – surely the people knew that the King's Son was about to get married? But there is also grief for the Son. Clearly, these people, his future subjects, don't care enough about him to want to share in his rejoicing. What's he got to do with us, they say? He won't make our businesses run. He won't generate an income for us. Their rejection of the Son is both personal and corporate. They reject not just him, but also their share in the future of the nation that he represents.

But the other source of anger in the story comes out of the sense

116

of urgency. Twice (verses 4 and 8) the King says that everything is 'ready'. It cannot wait, it will not keep, it's now or never. Why don't the invited guests realize? They will never again get the chance to go to a royal wedding.

The three parables, from 21.28 to this one, are all about the way in which Jesus's audience are passing up their chance to share in the kingdom. The stories get more and more pointed, making it clearer and clearer that all of this focuses on Jesus. Jesus and the kingdom of God go together – to reject one is to reject the other. It is clear from the way that they react to all three of the stories that the Pharisees understand what is being said, and that it is directed towards them: it's just that they don't believe it. They do not believe that this ordinary human being, standing before them, taking liberties with the tradition that they alone understand and are authorized to interpret, has their lives in his hand. They do not believe that their reaction to him will decide their fates. Would you have done? Or are you, by any chance, the man without a wedding robe?

It is terribly hard to feel that this man is being treated fairly. After all, he didn't know he was going to be invited, and if the rest of the guests were picked up off the streets, how well dressed were any of them? You imagine this poor guest sitting there, eating as much as he can, filling up his cup steadily, not sure what he's doing there, but determined to make the most of it. Then all of a sudden, there's the King. The man is completely thrown. Perhaps he hadn't even realized where he was. He had just gone along with the crowd, eager for a free feed. He didn't know he was celebrating the Son's banquet. The King's initial question is quite friendly in tone. All kinds of possible responses might have allowed the man to stay at the banquet. He could have said, 'I could see how urgent it was, and I wanted to make sure I didn't miss it.' Or, 'I don't own a wedding gown, but I'd love to borrow one.' Instead, he is silent, and he loses his chance.

Like the people who rejected the initial invitation, this guest is not interested in his relationship with the King. He never expected or wanted to meet him or speak to him, and he doesn't care what the banquet is for. This is Matthew's sombre warning – unless we have come to rejoice with the Son, there is nothing for us here.

Proper 24

———— ∿ ————

Isaiah 45.1–7
1 Thessalonians 1.1–10
Matthew 22.15–22

The question as weapon is one of the oldest techniques in controversy. You will hear it used to perfection most mornings on the radio. The art is to find the question to which there is no acceptable answer, so that any response simply digs the answerer into deeper and deeper trouble. This, of course, changes the whole nature and purpose of a question, since the point of most questions is to elicit an answer, with the assumption that the one asking the questions does not know the answer and is then, in some sense, dependent upon the one who does. But the point of the unanswerable question is to put the questioner in a position of power.

The Pharisees are confident that they have found the perfect question to ask Jesus. Whichever way he answers this, he will alienate some of his followers, and that is exactly what the Pharisees want: they want to erode Jesus's power base, without dirtying their own hands. So, they calculate, if Jesus replies that taxes should be paid to the illegal Roman usurper, he will anger those of his followers who hope and believe that he is the Messiah, the one who will reassert God's direct rule over his people, and get rid of the Romans. But if he tries to please that group by saying that taxes should be withheld, he will be liable for arrest by the civil powers, and he will frighten off the ordinary people, who want no trouble with the authorities, but who just come to Jesus to hear about God and to find consolation and healing. 'Got him!' the Pharisees chortle.

But if they think their weasel words of flattery will lull Jesus into a false sense of security, they are quickly proved very wrong. Within seconds, they are the ones scrabbling for an answer, with their careful strategy completely destroyed. Once again, as in all their dealings with Jesus, they are made to look like fools, who do not know their own business. They are supposed to be the religious leaders, but they never thought to introduce the question of God's rights into the debate. It is Jesus who does that, as though he knows more about God than they do. And since that has always been the heart of their hatred for him, they go away with the situation completely unchanged, but their own anger growing to the point where it will not be contained for much longer.

It apparently does not occur to them that Jesus's answer is a real one, perhaps because their question was not real, and they didn't want an actual answer. But Matthew, through his careful placing of this story, and through the build-up of the question and answer, makes us pause. What does the answer mean? Commentators often dwell on the 'render to Caesar' part of the story, to abstract some kind of Christian response to a secularized authority. But it is not Caesar whom Jesus introduces into the conversation – he was put there by the Pharisees. The Pharisees are pretending to want guidance about our duty to 'Caesar', but they are patently refusing guidance from Jesus about our duty to God.

In Matthew's Gospel, this confrontation between Jesus and the Pharisees comes after a whole series of parables about people who refuse to give God his due, and who will not recognize and rejoice with his Son. So when the Son stands, now, in front of this group of religious leaders, and says, 'What do you think your duty to God might be?', the answer is plain. Their duty is to use all their supposed knowledge of God to recognize the Son, and allow others to do the same. But this is the one thing they are absolutely determined not to do.

Why? Why? Why? Why do they hate him so? What is it about Jesus that so challenges them? It is not enough to say that they thought he was a mad impostor. Jerusalem was full of mad religious impostors, but they did not require large conspiracies on the part of the Pharisees to remove them. No, the trouble with Jesus was precisely that they could not be sure that he was an impostor. It is hard to avoid the conclusion that they really did not want God to get that close. And they were right to fear. It would certainly be much easier if God were like Caesar, so that we knew for sure when we had paid our taxes. But if God is actually like Jesus, then we might need, painfully and humiliatingly, to recognize him over and over again, and give him everything, not just what we consider to be his share.

The Last Sunday After Trinity

———— ❧ ————

Leviticus 19.1–2, 15–18
1 Thessalonians 2.1–8
Matthew 22.34–46

1 Thessalonians is almost certainly the oldest document in the New Testament. As in so many other things, Paul is a pioneer. It is hard for us to imagine ourselves back to a time when the Christian community had no 'writings' of their own. But one of the things that the epistles make clear is that there was, nonetheless, a remarkable degree of certainty about what constituted the heart of the Christian faith. It centred around the death and resurrection of Jesus, as the activity of God, at work to rescue his people (cf. 1 Thess. 1.10).

These earliest Christians had the Jewish scriptures, which might not be at all well known to those who were Gentile converts, and they had the stories of Jesus told to them by their founders, and then some, the lucky ones, had letters. How Paul's letters must have been treasured by his churches, longing for reassurance and sustenance in their new life. Very few of the epistles in the New Testament are formal theological treatises. The nearest Paul comes to that is in Romans. Most were personal, though clearly meant to be read several times, aloud, to the gathered Christian community.

There are all kinds of things about this letter that mark it out as something designed to be read in a way that we are no longer familiar with. We can flip back a few pages in the Bible and read Acts 16 and 17 for the story of how Paul came to found the church in Thessalonica, but these first readers do not have that luxury. So Paul reminds them. You can imagine that the person who was reading the letter aloud to the group of Christians gathered – in someone's house, perhaps, or outside under a tree? – would have had to pause at this point.

'I remember that,' someone would say. 'Poor old Paul and Silas. Their preaching caused a riot in Philippi, and they ended up in prison. Then when they finally got away, they couldn't find anywhere else to settle for a bit. They were really exhausted when they landed up here.'

Christians who hadn't been present on that momentous visit would press for details. Some of them may even have become Christians after Paul had left, and they wanted to hear everything.

'Well, Paul stayed with Jason' – everyone turned to look at Jason, who went rather pink, but couldn't help being proud at the memory. 'And they started preaching round the synagogue, and lots of us realized that what they said made sense.'

'And lots of us,' chimed in the Gentile Christians. 'We'd always liked the sound of the Jewish God, but thought he wouldn't be interested in us. But now Paul told us that this Jesus showed us that God did want us too.'

'Well then,' continued the first speaker, 'some of the Jews didn't like the sound of what Paul was saying, and they came to get him.'

'Yes,' chuckled Jason. 'But they got me instead.'

'Good job you're rich, Jason,' teased one of the others. 'At least that way they only took your money.'

'Well, I got a good few bruises, as well,' retorted Jason. 'And then we managed to get Paul and Silas away.'

By this time, the gathered crowd of people are feeling glowing and pleased with themselves. They had believed when many hadn't, and they had helped to save their heroes. No wonder Paul was writing so warmly to them. Paul had put himself in danger to bring the gospel to them, and they had responded magnificently. He could absolutely rely on them.

This is a very clever tactic on Paul's part. There's nothing like a shared memory of triumph against adversity to bring a group closer together. How vital this kind of memory must have been for the small communities of the earliest Christians, facing hardship, struggling to maintain their distinctiveness. Only deep loyalty to Paul and to each other was going to keep their commitment to Christ going. How many times was this letter read by the Thessalonians, with every word and phrase being pondered and prayed over? How many times was it copied and recopied, over the years to come, so that it wouldn't wear out, so that it could be shared more widely, so that we, thousands of years later, could read the words of love and praise written by the Apostle Paul to the Christians in Thessalonica, within twenty years of the death and resurrection of Christ?

The Thessalonians were very aware of God's provision for them – he had sent them Paul, to preach the gospel. But even more, he sent his Son, the Word not just written, but incarnate.

Sundays Before Advent

The Fourth Sunday Before Advent

—— ⁓ ——

Micah 3.5–12
1 Thessalonians 2.9–13
Matthew 24.1–14

'That was a really depressing morning,' said one disciple to another, leaning back in the sparse shade of the olive tree to keep out of the midday sun.

'Yes,' agreed another. 'I'm thinking of packing it in. I can't see that he's ever going to show his hand and lead us all to power.'

'But that's just what he said would happen,' chipped in a third. 'He said that some of our hearts will grow cold, and that we'll stop being his followers.'

'He didn't mean *us*,' retorted the first disciple. 'As far as I could tell, he seems to think all of this could go on for generations, getting worse and worse.'

'And why does he have to keep annoying the Pharisees if he isn't going to take them on properly?' murmured the second disciple, discontentedly. 'He'll just get us all into trouble for no good reason.'

The little group sat back, hot and angry, contemplating the morning they had just had. First of all, Jesus had got into yet another slanging match with the Pharisees, one of the worst of the increasingly hostile encounters between them. Then, after they'd left the temple, followed by the buzz of furious and thrilled conversation, Jesus turned back and looked at the sacred beloved building, and said, 'It won't last much longer.'

Well, of course, that raised a lot of hopes. After all, the only way they could manage without the temple was if God was going to come and rule directly. So that meant that Jesus was at last ready to overthrow the Romans and the Jewish leaders who opposed him, and reign directly for God.

'When, when?' the disciples asked eagerly, hoping for an exact date, like 'next week', or 'at the Passover', or something definite.

But instead, what they got was a long list of things that had to happen first, all of them horrible, many of them painful to the very disciples who were ready to sacrifice everything for Jesus's cause.

Except, of course, they weren't ready. They might have been prepared to take up arms, if it came to it, though they were secretly hoping that enough of the people would come over to their side to make it unnecessary. But what Jesus seemed to be suggesting was that many of them would use up their lives, and die horrible deaths, and still see nothing. They also couldn't help noticing that Jesus kept saying things like 'They will hand *you* over', or '*You* will hear of wars', almost as though he wasn't going to be with them in it.

The only clue Jesus gave them about actual timing was that the end was linked to the spreading of the good news of the kingdom throughout the world. 'What good news?' they asked each other. 'I didn't hear any good news in what he just said.'

'Yes,' laughed one of them, going off into a parody of a popular preacher. 'Join my wonderful movement, and you might end up hating each other and getting killed. That message is going to catch on.'

And yet, amazingly, the good news of the kingdom of the crucified Messiah did catch on. Despite all temptations and occasional failures, most of those first disciples did endure to the end, and did persuade thousands of others that the kingdom of the risen Lord is the country that they have always longed for, a country where God directly rules his subjects, with justice and love held together.

When it is Paul's turn to preach this gospel, he gives us a little vignette of his methods in Thessalonica. He settles down with the people, earning his own living, trying to live out and embody that vision of a righteousness that is loving and converting. Above all, he doesn't want the Thessalonians to think of the gospel as something only he can give them. He is delighted that through his preaching they recognize God's greatness, not Paul's.

But if this is a brief pastoral idyll for Paul, there are many more scenes of violence and pain. Intrinsic to Jesus's message, as Paul and the disciples know so well, is the cost. The cost is borne first of all and supremely by Jesus himself, but this good news, of the direct reign of God, sweeping away all the false gods and false rulers we so busily build in God's place, can never be preached without warnings. If this costs you, will you still hear it as good news? Do you want the closeness of God more than anything? Only God can make this good news, because only God is supremely worth it. Our job is to get out of the way, so that we can become channels, like Paul, for God's word.

The Third Sunday Before Advent

—— ～ ——

Amos 5.18–24
1 Thessalonians 4.13–18
Matthew 25.1–13

These are odd Sundays, these ones before Advent. We are preparing to be prepared, getting ready to get ready, and all the readings are agreed that this is quite a sombre business. What is the best way to use this period of inaction, before the bustle really begins?

Matthew's Gospel suggests this is a good time to lay in provisions, and make sure that your oil supplies will last through any emergency. But perhaps verse 11 also suggests that this is a good time to familiarize yourself with what it is that you are looking forward to, so that you will recognize it when it comes, and, more importantly, it will recognize you. These flighty bridesmaids haven't bothered to get in enough oil for their lamps because they don't, at heart, care very much about the wedding they are going to. They don't seem to have paid visits to the couple and their family beforehand, or bought them an engagement present, or done anything suggesting that the bridegroom is actually a friend. They just want to turn up for the party. With better preparation, they might not have been treated as gatecrashers.

Amos, too, suggests that you should use as much of your time as possible familiarizing yourself with God, and not just looking forward to the party, without caring whose party it really is, or what kind of present he would really like.

Amos is talking to a group of his fellow-countrymen who have lost sight of what God is really like. They use religious language and rituals freely, and enjoy them, and they are confident that God is a chum of theirs. So they are quite looking forward, they think, to God's big party, the day of the Lord. They don't mind if it doesn't come too soon, since they are quite comfortable as they are, but they have no real worries about their relationship with God.

Into this well-off gentlemen's club kind of atmosphere Amos's words are hurled, and they scorch and burn everything they touch.

126

Amos reminds them that their primary purpose in life is to be God's covenant people, living a shared life that reflects what God really cares about. Sadly, the people have forgotten to do their regular checks on what God is really like. They have assumed that God must like what they would like, which is lots of attention and praise, and lavish ceremonies of which he is the centre. What God wants is a community of righteousness and justice, Amos thunders, where no one is performing easy religious ceremonies and going home to a large dinner, while other people starve.

Verse 24 is often sung as though it was something to look forward to, but read it carefully and what you see is the destructive violence of a huge torrent of water, sweeping away everything in its path. The puny little grain offerings and burnt offerings will vanish without trace, and the people will be left clinging helplessly to the mercy of the God they barely know any more.

The way the prophets of the Old Testament hammer home the message of God's fierce determination to shape a people of justice and righteousness should give us all pause. It is very unlikely that God has suddenly stopped caring about these things that have always been central to his communication with his people.

And if the reading from Thessalonians comes as a relief after all that doom and gloom, perhaps we should be careful to read it in context. The Thessalonians are, Paul tells us, people who have been preparing hard to be ready for the Lord. They have done everything they can to make sure that they recognize him and are recognized by him. They have accepted the gospel preached to them by Paul, and they have realized that it has implications for their life together. They are trying so hard to live in love and justice with one another. So to them, Paul can give some assurances. God is faithful, and for those who have shaped themselves according to his nature, the coming of God is good news. No doors will be slammed in their faces, and no floods will wash them away.

Preparing to be prepared involves looking back over God's dealings with us, so that we will know and be known. 'When our gratitude for the past is only partial, our hope for a new future can never be full . . . If we are to be truly ready for a new task in the service of God, our entire past, gathered into the spaciousness of a converted heart, must become the source of energy that moves us toward the future', writes Henri Nouwen.[1]

---

[1] Henri Nouwen, 'All is Grace', *Weavings*, December 1992.

The Second Sunday Before Advent

—— ≈ ——

Zephaniah 1.7, 12–18
1 Thessalonians 5.1–11
Matthew 25.14–30

The word 'gospel' means 'good news', and Christians believe that, in Jesus Christ, the whole world is offered the good news of God's love for them. But the New Testament also bears witness to the fact that not everyone receives God's love as 'good news'. Incredible as it may seem, some people look at Jesus and hate him and the God he represents. Some feel threatened, some feel bored, some hate the way he breaks their rules about God, and some simply do not recognize what is on offer. The passages that the lectionary gives us to reflect upon in these Sundays before Advent are all full of foreboding and warning. It is possible to reject the love of God, and so to reject your own life. It is possible to live in such a way that you do not recognize Life when it stands in front of you.

Zephaniah describes a people characterized by the word 'complacent' (v. 12). They believe that they have a good life because it is materially comfortable. They are well housed and well fed, and they believe that they can keep God at a safe distance. After all, their wealth has enabled them to keep all other uncomfortable things at bay so why not God too? It's not that they don't believe in God, it's just that they think they have bought his neutrality – he won't intervene, one way or another.

To them, God comes as a hostile and destructive army, taking away all their security and giving them only terror. There is no 'good news' for them, because the only good news they would recognize is no news. They don't want to hear anything about God at all. Unfortunately, in God's world, that is not an option.

The slave in Matthew's parable is not quite that far gone. He knows the master quite well, but he fears and dislikes him. We have no idea what has led to this state of affairs between master and slave. Obviously, the master is a bit of a maverick. Not many masters would give their slaves quantities of money, and go off for

128

an unspecified period of time, to an unknown destination, leaving no instructions. He doesn't tell the slaves what they are expected to do with the property but, clearly, he knows them quite well, and they know him. They know that this is a test of some kind, and they approach it each in his own way.

The slave who is given one talent already believes that the master doesn't think much of him. There may be a longer history to this than we are told, but it is obvious to him that the master trusts him less than the others, because he gives him less. And this slave is both afraid and resentful. His resentment comes bubbling out when the master finally returns, and the slave finds himself pouring out what he really thinks of the master. He knows he's going to get into trouble, but he's determined to have his say first.

The master's response is interesting. He recognizes the slave's description of himself, but not why it led to that result. 'If you're so scared of me,' the master says, 'why didn't you try harder to please me?'

And to this, the slave has no answer. He had decided, long ago, that nothing he did would please his master, and he has given up trying.

To this man, God is not 'good news' because he is too obsessed with his own failure. He cannot see that all the other slaves are rewarded for their efforts, irrespective of whether they earned big profits or small. He has turned his own failure into a weapon. 'This is your fault, God,' he shouts, 'not mine.' He cannot recognize good news because he doesn't actually know himself at all. In order to hear good news, you have to have some idea of what would constitute good news for your situation. But this slave is only looking for the downside of everything. He doesn't want any good news, because he's sure there will be a drawback in it somewhere.

The Thessalonians want God's good news, though even they are slightly apprehensive about it. This good news is not something to take lightly. You have to be prepared for it, live your life in anticipation of it, stick together and help each other train for it.

Why should the 'good news' of the love of God be so alarming? Perhaps because few of us actually know how to be loved. We know how to be pampered, or to indulge ourselves, or to whine about being misunderstood. But to be loved with God's total, consuming, transforming and utterly perceptive love? Are we ready for that?

Christic the King

—— ∿ ——

Ezekiel 34.11–16, 20–4
Ephesians 1.15–23
Matthew 25.31–46

Matthew 25 is all about preparedness. First of all, there are the
foolish bridesmaids, who ran out of oil and so missed the wedding;
then there is the slave who wasted his chance of increasing his one
talent while the master was away, and now we have the sheep and
the goats. All of these people and groups are unprepared for what
is about to happen, and they face terrible consequences, for the
stories are not just about the importance of being ready, but also
about judgement. The people in the stories make their judgements.
The foolish bridesmaids decide there is no great rush. The slave
with one talent decides to do nothing, and the 'goats' decide that
some people are not worth bothering about. God then makes his
judgement and, unfortunately, it is completely different from theirs.

All the people standing at the throne of glory are taken aback by
God's judgement and, more particularly, by God's judge. They were
not expecting to see the Son of Man up there on the throne, looking
completely at home, with angels around him carrying on as if they
thought he was God. As the people are separated into two groups,
one on the right hand and one on the left of this awesome yet recognizable figure, it is clear that both groups are equally puzzled. They
are both, you might say, unprepared for this standard of judgement.
Neither group had lived their lives expecting to have them judged
by this Man, in this way. As their sentences are handed down, both
groups say, 'We didn't know we would be judged for *that*.'

The judge does not explain himself, but he could have pointed to
both the law and the prophets, which make it clear what God
expects. The reading from Ezekiel, for example, shows God himself
looking for the lost sheep and longing to care for them. It also
shows God's judgement on those 'fat sheep' who kept the pasture
for themselves, and deliberately pushed away the hungry and the
needy. Any well-brought-up Jew listening to Jesus's parable of the

130

sheep and the goats would recognize the justice of the judgement handed out to the goats. No one could say that they were not warned about the nature of God.

So how did they – and how do we – manage so to be deceived? How did we manage to persuade ourselves that there would be no real consequences for the way we live? As we gorge ourselves to death, how come we do not realize that we are the fat sheep, pushing the starving millions away from our green fields?

That is what makes the Son of Man such a terrible judge. Judgement is not something alien and distant, but something that bears the human face of the neglected, the tortured, the crucified. God is not far away, and not easy to deceive, and we cannot plead that we did not know what he wanted of us. We know perfectly well what the hungry, thirsty, estranged, naked, sick and imprisoned people around us want. Jesus the Son of Man is to be our judge, and the human face he shows us is all too recognizable.

That is why Paul's prayer for the Ephesians is that they might come to know Jesus Christ. On the face of it, Ephesians and the parable of the sheep and the goats could not be more different. The parable has often been read as meaning that you don't need to be religious to please God. Although the Judge in the story is Jesus, the King, the Son of Man, it is certainly true that the sheep didn't think they recognized him in those whom they helped. They did their good deeds without any ulterior motives, looking for no recognition. Whereas the knowledge of God that the Ephesians have sounds like theoretical knowledge, issuing in no particular kind of behaviour, and with the obvious hope of rich reward in heaven.

But if you look more closely, that is far from the truth. This 'knowledge' is the knowledge that God's revelation is to be found in the crucified Jesus, and that this human, suffering figure is the one who rules for God, and to whom all creation is subject. When we, his Church, acknowledge him as our King, and become his body, we can have no illusions about what that body looks like. We believe in God's great power, at work in Jesus, to bring life out of death. And so we, his body, work to bring life out of the death all around us. We work to pay attention to the real human beings with whom God came to identify, and we look around us for the life that created and redeemed out of love.

The Society for Promoting Christian Knowledge (SPCK) was founded in 1698. Its mission statement is:

To promote Christian knowledge by
- **Communicating the Christian faith in its rich diversity;**
- **Helping people to understand the Christian faith and to develop their personal faith; and**
- **Equipping Christians for mission and ministry.**

SPCK Worldwide serves the Church through Christian literature and communication projects in over 100 countries, and provides books for those training for ministry in many parts of the developing world. This worldwide service depends upon the generosity of others and all gifts are spent wholly on ministry programmes, without deductions.

SPCK Bookshops support the life of the Christian community by making available a full range of Christian literature and other resources, providing support for those training for ministry, and assisting bookstalls and book agents throughout the UK.

SPCK Publishing produces Christian books and resources, covering a wide range of inspirational, pastoral, practical and academic subjects. Authors are drawn from many different Christian traditions, and publications aim to meet the needs of a wide variety of readers in the UK and throughout the world.

The Society does not necessarily endorse the individual views contained in its publications, but hopes they stimulate readers to think about and further develop their Christian faith.

For further information about the Society, visit our website at *www.spck.org.uk,* or write to:
SPCK, Holy Trinity Church, Marylebone Road,
London NW1 4DU, United Kingdom.